Crossings

McCullough's Coastal Bridges

Maps

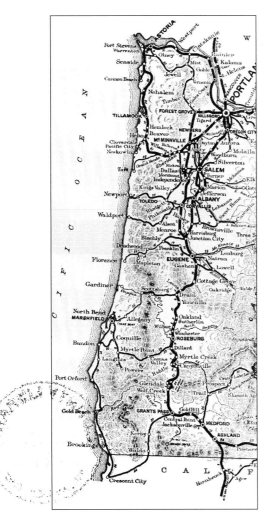

A map of Oregon from 1919 (left) shows a huge gap in the Coast Highway from Neskowin on the north to North Bend on the south coast. The completed highway (right) after the construction of the coastal bridges shows the connection between Astoria on the north to Brookings–Harbor and California on the south.

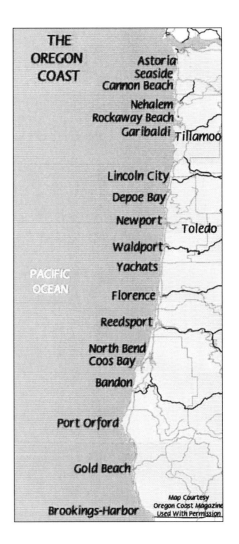

Crossings

MᶜCULLOUGH'S COASTAL BRIDGES

JUDY FLEAGLE • RICHARD KNOX SMITH

Judy Fleagle

*The right man
at the right place
at the right time.*

PACIFIC PUBLISHING • FLORENCE • OREGON

Pacific Publishing
Florence • Oregon

Photo and illustration credits on page 223

Book design by Robert Serra / Pacific Publishing
Cover photos front and back of Siuslaw River Bridge
by Robert Serra
Production Assistance by Patrick Looney

Text formatted in Baskerville and Arial

Library of Congress Control Number: 2011923001

ISBN: 9780615449210

Distributed by
Pacific Publishing
P.O. Box 2767 • 327 Laurel Street
Florence • Oregon • 97439
(541) 997-1040 • pacpub@oregonfast.net

Third Edition
2012

Contents

"As the focus of my interest in bridges is based primarily upon their aesthetic appeal, it is only natural that I am often asked to identify my favorite bridge. There is such a wide variety of bridge types and so many wonderful examples of each that I find it impossible to come up with a single answer. . . . I do, however, have some favorite categories. First, the pride of my own state [Oregon], the unique and varied bridges of Conde B. McCullough."

— Robert S. Cortright —

Author

Bridging: Discovering the Beauty of Bridges

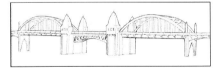

Foreword

~~~~

MY INTRODUCTION to the Siuslaw River Bridge, a McCullough bridge, took place 75 years ago. I was part of a Boy Scout drum-and-bugle corps from Cottage Grove that came to Florence for the dedication. We rode over on the back of a flatbed truck and enjoyed an overnight camp out. I can't imagine anyone today hauling a bunch of boys almost 200 miles round-trip on the back of a truck.

Memories of the trip are hazy. I have a fuzzy snapshot of three friends at the end of the bridge and a copy of the souvenir program. My fondest memory is of the salmon dinner that was held under the bridge. The aroma of it cooking drew my pals and me to the line . . . more than once. The salmon had been rolled in cracker crumbs and was deep-fried. I had eaten a lot of salmon, but this was so good I convinced my mom to try it.

Fast-forward 50 years. My wife, Harriet, and I moved to Florence just in time for the 50th anniversary celebration of the Siuslaw River Bridge. I remember that I attended an event at the Siuslaw Pioneer Museum, featuring locals that had been present at the bridge's dedication.

These contacts were in mind when in 2006 I had to prepare a major "paper" for a discussion group. We could choose our own topic, so I chose the Siuslaw River Bridge. By that time, the bridge had become a familiar friend, taking me safely across the Siuslaw River on my way to and from home to town and back. We still average at least two round trips a day.

My selection of the bridge projected me into some major research. Since Harriet's father had been a bridge engineer, she was interested and joined me on my trips. We visited McCullough's 12 bridges on the coast, spoke with folks at Mercer–Fraser Company — the construction firm that built the bridge — in Eureka, California, explored the records at the library at Oregon State University in Corvallis, searched newspaper files at the Knight Library at the University of Oregon in Eugene, and were guided through the mysteries of the State of Oregon Archives in Salem.

We found a warm welcome at each point of contact because the McCullough bridges are treasured by a wide variety of people for many reasons.

More than a dozen audiences saw my resulting PowerPoint presentation. It was timely because the Siuslaw River Bridge would soon be receiving the first major renovation since it was built. The Oregon Department of Transportation's efforts in 2009–2010 have brought a new sparkle to the bridge just in time to celebrate its 75th birthday.

In honor of this milestone, Judy Fleagle has expanded on my efforts by weaving together a two-part tale of how the bridge, along with four other historic coastal bridges, came to be built and what makes our bridge so special. This book is basically a love story. I wish the Siuslaw River Bridge a grand celebration and many more years of service. Happy birthday to one of the most beloved bridges on the coast!

— *Richard Knox "Dick" Smith* —

~~~

THIS BOOK IS DEDICATED TO . . .

numerous Florence old-timers

who searched their memories

while my tape recorder was running,

and

my sister, Edna,

steadfast friends, and Jan and Sharon of my critique group

who showered me with encouragement . . .

once I finally got started.

— *JUDY FLEAGLE* —

Preface

~~~~~~

THIS BOOK is a joint venture between historian and researcher Dick Smith and myself. Without his research, this book would not exist. He spent an entire year on the project, which resulted in a PowerPoint presentation enjoyed by many.

His passion for the Siuslaw River Bridge, the bridge's designer Conde B. McCullough, and the history behind the building of the bridge and Highway 101 piqued my interest, and when he asked me to help transform it into a book in 2007, I felt honored and couldn't say no.

But I was tempted to say no, when I first saw the piles of books, hundreds of copies of historic newspaper articles, CDs from state agencies with photos, charts, and expense receipts, other miscellaneous materials, and the PowerPoint CD that he had provided to help me in the writing. This was a busy time in my life and this research documentation sat in boxes and file drawers for the next 2 1/2 years while I finished my career as writer/editor at two Northwest magazines. Then in mid-2009 I retired, which enabled me to complete long-delayed house projects and to deal with family obligations. At last, by January 2010 I felt ready.

As I delved into the project, I was struck by the convergence of the need for the coastal bridges just at the time that Conde B. McCullough, Oregon's greatest bridge builder, reached the peak of his genius, and just when financial help was available from the federal government through Roosevelt's New Deal. This convergence provided the perfect storm for bridge building on the Oregon Coast — the 1934 through 1936 Oregon Coast Bridges Project that resulted in five fabulous bridges.

Then Dick loaned me *Bridges: A History of the World's Most Famous and Important Spans,* a book by Judith Dupre that profiles 50 of the world's greatest bridges. And the Siuslaw River Bridge counts as one because it represents the bridges of Conde B. McCullough. This bridge in Florence, while not as large or as well known as some of his other bridges, is one of the best at showcasing his innovative design techniques and characteristic aesthetic details.

Finally, the timing for a book about the Siuslaw River Bridge couldn't be better. 2010 marked the completion of the first major renovation since the bridge's completion in 1936. And 2011 marks its 75th birthday, as well as the birthdays of the other bridges of the Coast Bridges Project. How could I not do my part in getting this book published at this time!

— *Judy Fleagle* —

BOOK I

~~~~

Getting It Right

Conde B. McCullough Memorial Bridge over Coos Bay.

THROUGHOUT HISTORY there are examples of the right person at the right place at the right time. When that happens, amazing results take place. And that's exactly what occurred on the Oregon coast during a most improbable time — the Great Depression. Here is the story behind five of the coast's iconic bridges and their designer Conde B. McCullough, one of the greatest bridge designers of all time.

Jumping Off

The first automobile trip on the coast used mostly the beaches at low tide. The trip took place in 1912 involving four young men in a new Studebaker who drove from Newport to Siletz Bay (the southern edge of today's Lincoln City). It took an incredible 22 hours and 40 minutes as well as numerous tools to cover the 47-mile round trip.

PART I
THE PLACE: THE OREGON COAST

~~~~~

INTRODUCTION
Highway Beginnings

LIVING ON the Oregon coast prior to 1900 meant living in isolation with no roads connecting the communities north and south. Railroad lines connected a few towns to the inland valley, but for most communities the rivers were the highway — the main means of transportation east and west. To travel almost anywhere involved water. Ferries crossed rivers and coastal steamers provided transport up and down the coast. They were often the easiest means of transportation. Even after the turn of the century, wagons and stages were in use, but automobiles were few and far between.

Prior to 1913, each county constructed segments of road and any small bridges piecemeal as funds became available. A hodge-podge of roads existed mostly leading from the towns, but no coastal highway plan existed. On the north coast a rough road connected Astoria and Tillamook,

Ben Jones, from Lincoln County, became known as the "Father of the Coast Highway."

and on the south coast the Coos Bay Wagon Road connected Coos Bay area with Roseburg. The rugged central coast had no roads at all except within towns.

The book *Pathfinder* provides detailed descriptions of the first automobile trip on the coast using mostly the beaches at low tide. The trip took place in 1912 involving four young men in a new Studebaker who drove from Newport to Siletz Bay (the southern edge of today's Lincoln City). It took an incredible 22 hours and 40 minutes as well as numerous tools to cover the 47-mile round trip.

In 1913, Governor Oswald West declared — through executive order — that Oregon beaches were public highways. Before long, folks started seeing horse-drawn buggies and stages as well as the new-fangled automobiles on the beaches, since they provided the only connection between some towns.

Also in 1913, the state legislature created the Oregon State Highway Commission (OSHC) and the Oregon State Highway Department (OSHD) to — as the commission's slogan said — "Get Oregon Out of the Mud." This legislation put road- and bridge-building authority in the hands of the state. Although it makes sense now, back then groups such as the Grange and the Oregon State Federation of Labor opposed using tax dollars to build scenic highways for "the privileged few" and wanted the commission to be abolished and authority returned to the counties. Of course, that didn't happen.

In 1919, Oregon enacted the first gasoline tax in the country and this gave new life to the "good roads" campaign that was spreading across the country. Building the Pacific Highway from Portland through the Willamette, Umpqua, and Rogue valleys to the California state line confirmed Oregon's commitment to good roads.

Folks living on the coast wanted a highway too, connecting the coastal towns. Ben Jones, from Lincoln County, became an early leader of lobbying efforts to build a coastal highway. As a young man, he had served as a mail car-

rier on the central coast and experienced firsthand the primitive nature of the roads. Years later as a state representative, he wrote the first bill for the construction of the Oregon Coast Highway (HB 147) in 1919 and became known as the "Father of the Coast Highway." The legislation placed a measure before the voters, authorizing construction of a road from Astoria to the California state line. It would be known as the Roosevelt Coast Military

Digging Out

A member of the first coast "road" trip digs the Studebaker out of the mud.

4

Highway.

At this time, shortly after the end of World War I, voters approved a $2.5 million bond obligation, with expectations of federal matching funds. But the matching funds never materialized, and the state's authority to sell the bonds lapsed. After many twists and turns through the state legislature, it was on again by 1921. The state had permission to authorize the bonds — minus the federal funds — and the highway commission designated the Roosevelt Coast Military Highway a state highway with improvements authorized.

Finally, road construction began in earnest. Steve Wyatt in the *Bayfront Book* wrote that a Lincoln County newspaper from 1923 reported, "Practically every man and boy over fourteen years of age is employed on this road in some capacity, while most of the women are milking cows and doing chores."

The improvements came just in the nick of time — World War I was over and automobiles had become commonplace. By the early 1920s, Oregonians clamored for highway access to the coast. And, of course, folks who lived there simply wanted to be able to travel by car between towns.

Cars on the Beach

In the 1920s, Oregonians traveled to the coast as automobiles became more affordable.

River Crossing

Ferries played a large role in early coastal commerce. This "people" ferry crossed between Florence and Glenada in the distance. Notice the line connecting the boat to the scow.

CHAPTER 1

〜

Early Travel

WHILE TODAY we measure driving time from Astoria to the California state line in hours, in the mid-1920s, the trip was measured in days. And if someone said, "Don't leave home without it!" They wouldn't be thinking about a credit card, they would be thinking about a shovel. Even after five years of construction on the Roosevelt Coast Military Highway, travelers were still digging out of the mud if they ventured very far north or south of town.

Between stretches of new highway, travelers drove around headlands on unpaved narrow wagon roads, over marshy or sandy areas on planked roads, or upon the hard-packed sand of the beaches. Traveling very far along the Oregon coast in the mid-1920s was still quite an adventure where more than one shovel was often needed. That certainly was true for Arthur D. Sullivan, automobile editor of *The Oregonian*, and Ed Knox, representative of the Howard Automobile Company, during their historic trip down the Oregon coast.

Automobile tackles entire coast

Sullivan and Knox began their trip on a rainy September day in 1926. The road from Astoria to Taft (part of Lincoln City today) showed signs of progress. It was either completed, graded and waiting for surfacing, or in the process of being graded. As they neared Siletz Bay, they saw a bridge ahead still under construction, so they returned to Taft and took a detour through Kernville. Heavy rain had made the road too slippery to drive. "With the aid of a pair of chains, the Buick pulled herself through, dropped down into Kernville, and was ferried across the river there," wrote Sullivan.

They found their way back to the new highway and Knox had just finished saying, "Why man alive, nobody otta kick about this road!" when they drove into a mud hole on a segment that had not been surfaced yet. Before they knew it, they were up to the hubs and running boards in mud. Out came the shovels.

Even so, they made it to Newport on that first day with few

Crossing Over

A wooden bridge and plank road just south of Depoe Bay escort early travelers at Rocky Creek circa 1915. It was not replaced until 1927.

other problems. The central coast, however, portended a different story. There were long stretches of no road, which is where the beach came in handy. Then there were the intimidating headlands of Cape Perpetua and Heceta Head as well as the inhospitable dunes south of Florence. Travel between Newport and the Coos Bay area was anything but easy.

Sullivan and Knox ferried across the Alsea, traveled along the beach for a while after a long wait for the tide to go out, and left the sand near Yachats. Then for almost 40 miles, they traveled over a wild and rough road. "Little has been done in the way of maintenance," wrote Sullivan. "The road, due to slides, slopes precariously outward. It has no idea of federal standards of grades or curvature, and pursues its reckless way without regard for modern engineering along the bleak cliffs that mark the coastline."

And not long after they made it past Cape Perpetua, they were faced with Heceta Head.

The uphill grade, full of long, deep ruts, made driving almost impossible. They stopped and kicked brush and twigs into the mud and make a run for the top of the hill. After reaching it, "we wound along, in and out of ravines at a dizzy height above the sea," continued Sullivan. "We started downward over a series of abrupt curves and steep grades and gained sea level." After several winding miles through forests, they came upon the 6-mile stretch of new highway north of Florence, which must have seemed quite wonderful after the hard going of the headlands.

South of Florence the drive continued to be miserable because of the rainy weather and all the mud and deep puddles in the road. About 10 miles south of town on a long, steep climb,

they became high-centered due to such deep ruts. Their wheels spun, but they went nowhere.

They commandeered fence rails to pry the car back onto the road. After that was accomplished, they started cutting brush to fill in the deep ruts on the steep slope. "The roadbed was slippery," wrote Sullivan. "So slippery that our feet acquired the bad habit of going out from under us on the slightest provocation." After a couple of hours of work, they were able to charge over their newly built road and over the hill.

Then for the next three hours, they couldn't seem to get above 5 or 10 miles per hour and geysers of muddy water kept shooting up around them from all the puddles they were driving through. They even lost a chain and didn't even realize it until they headed up the next incline and discovered they had no power. "We started back through the mud, the muck, and the mire and after a two-mile hike, found the lost chain," wrote Sullivan.

The shovels came in handy whenever they ran into slides, which were regular occurrences with all the rain on steep hillsides. Between the slides, skidding on slippery surfaces, and bouncing from one deep rut to another, it was a battle. "We literally 'fought' our way for every inch of that 20-mile stretch," wrote Sullivan. When they were only a mile from Gardiner, they came upon a new section and coasted down to the ferry dock on the Umpqua River shortly after 1 a.m.

Once there, they had to spend a couple of hours rousting out a ferryman. They succeeded and he got them to Reedsport just as dawn was breaking. It had been a long day and night.

Because of road construction south of town on the new highway, they boarded a scow that was tied alongside the tug *Juno III*

On the Road at High Tide

A swamped early motorist navigates the coast road, but not without a hitch. Horses to the rescue was not uncommon.

to ferry them to the beach south of Winchester Bay. But only a short distance from the dock, they had to stop for about an hour to pump water out of the scow. After becoming seaworthy, the captain got them to Winchester Bay and even ran the scow up on a sandbank for them. But when Sullivan and Knox got off and laid out planks for a roadway, they found the sand was too soft for an automobile.

Another frustration, but it didn't stop them. Knox lowered the pressure in the tires, took a run for it, and made it a short distance before getting stuck. They used planks to make a roadway and the Buick dug itself out. Knox got into firmer sand and made quite some headway before getting stuck again. This time after an hour of shoveling and pushing, they realized they needed help. So they looked around and spotted a team of horses at a logging camp across the mud flats of Winchester Bay. Sullivan hotfooted it over, and after much discussion, convinced the logging crew to spare a man and team of horses.

When they got back with the horses, the car had sunk up to its hubs. But with the horses pulling and Knox applying gas, the Buick lurched out and away until they hit the firmer sand of a dune and they were able to continue on to the hard sands of the beach. Then they unhitched the horses and gratefully thanked the logging crew. They continued on. "Over the smooth beach, we rolled along at 30, 35, 40 miles an hour," wrote Sullivan.

They could have gone farther, but they parked the car above the high tide line and headed inland to scout out an old road, which their government maps indicated was nearby and could connect them to the next section of finished highway. Driving on the completed segments comprised one of the goals of their trip. Their scouting didn't result in finding a road — just endless dunes. About the time they decided to walk to the next town, Lakeside, they stumbled upon a house and small farm where an elderly farmer said that he and his team of white mares could help since they had just rescued another car a couple days before.

A short time later, a strange group ventured forth. "In the lead was the farmer's dog. Then came the farmer, long stick in hand, hunting for the hard spots in the sand. Then the team of white mares, the wagon, and hitched to the wagon was the Buick," wrote Sullivan. "Two hours work, though, got us to one end of a county road." They paid the farmer for his help, pumped up the tires, and were glad to be out of the dunes. It had taken 17 hours to get from Reedsport to the Coos Bay ferry landing. (Today a trip of about 25 minutes.)

From Coos Bay south, the Buick rolled along mostly on new highway — the ride blissfully uneventful. They spent the night at Bandon and continued on the last leg of the trip in the morning. They didn't run into an unsurfaced grade until near Gold Beach, and at the Rogue River they boarded the last of the ferries. The winding rough road over Pistol Mountain constituted the most difficult section of this last leg, and then it dropped down near Brookings onto a finished section of the new highway. Finally, it was into California and before long the intersection of the Roosevelt and Redwood highways — the end of their journey. It had taken four days — 57 hours of driving time — to travel from Astoria to Crescent City by automobile. Sullivan and Knox, in spite of numerous hardships, became the first to drive the entire Oregon coast.

Bus travels entire coast

Improvements happened so fast, that by the next year, buses serviced the coast. Compared to today's big comfortable coaches, these early ones rate as quite primitive.

Ricki Derrickson remembers. In 1927, when she was a little girl, she traveled with her mother by bus from Tacoma, Washington, to Los Angeles, and she didn't think much of the stretch through Oregon. She described Oregon's Roosevelt Highway as "a muddy wagon track" with construction all along the way. A few miles south of Florence, the bus somehow got stuck between the burning ends of a tree. "We all got off and so did the driver," wrote Derrickson. "He waded through the mud to a bulldozer.

Then he got on, started it up, brought it down to the bus, hooked it on, and pulled it free. We boarded the bus and were on our way."

When they got to the next town and had unloaded the baggage, they discovered that some pieces had been damaged. "Our satchel had been scorched," she wrote. "In the bag was my Teddy bear — both ears singed. I was devastated, but loved him all the more for surviving his painful experience. I still have him [1995], scorched ears and all."

The new highway improvements continued — especially on the north and south coasts, but travel on the central coast continued to be a problem for both travelers and residents.

Taking the bus

This old bus would be similar to the one Ricki Derrickson rode while traveling the coast in 1927.

CHAPTER 2

〜〜〜

The Isolated Central Coast

A 1919 ROAD MAP showing the Oregon coast does not even show any roads between Neskowin all the way to North Bend. According to *The Florence Book* by Ed Pursley, "By 1925, the Roosevelt Coast Military Highway was completed in Oregon except for 90 miles in the middle." Even by the end of the 1920s, the central coast remained isolated with long detours between the new road segments. New small bridges crossed streams, but on the tidal estuaries of the major rivers, ferries were still a way of life.

A second historic car trip showed that eight years after the beginning of construction on the Roosevelt Highway, good roads on the central coast were still missing between Newport and Florence.

First attempt at driving the coast in a day

In 1929, a four-member team with two cars took the same trip leaving on the same September day as Sullivan and Knox three years before, and one of them again bore the designation of automobile editor at *The Oregonian*. This time it was Lawrence Barber who documented the trip for the newspaper, and a few of his quotes are used here.

On this second trip, the team wanted to prove that while automobile travel had improved since the 1926 trip along the Roosevelt Highway, it still had a ways to go before it could be considered "navigable."

Besides Barber, the team included Roy Conway, representing the Oregon State Motor Association; Charles E. Nims, representing the national Portland Cement Association; and John H. Weiser, representing Marquette automobiles. They would be driving two cars on this trip: a new 1929 Marquette touring car from a Buick–Marquette dealership in Portland and a Buick sedan owned by Nims "who was interested in selling cement for road building."

This time the weather was dry and they were attempting to complete it within a 24-hour period to become the first car to drive the entire coast in a day. Because the road between Astoria and Newport had been surfaced with macadam — small gravel often bound by tar or asphalt — the two cars drove it in little more than four hours. That was excellent time, but the Yaquina

Heceta Head

To see Heceta Head Lighthouse situated on a bare, treeless headland is a strange sight today. In the 1920s, though, sheep grazed on the grassy headland.

Bay ferry in Newport was only the first of six ferry crossings, all of which would slow them down.

Just south of Yaquina Bay, they ran out of good roads. First, they encountered a corduroy road, consisting of planks or logs that had been laid side by side over soft, sandy ground, that involved very careful driving. Next, they drove on the beach to Seal Rock. Then more corduroy road, back to the beach, and finally, they ended up driving on a nerve-racking single lane timber trestle elevated 15 feet above the sand for a quarter mile to the ferry landing. The tracks on the trestle were flanged on the inside to keep the tires on. Nevertheless, they must have been mighty glad to leave that behind. The ferry crossing at Alsea Bay took only about 15 minutes, but numerous detours slowed them down on the stretch to Yachats.

On the 33-mile route between Yachats and Florence, the two cars had an exciting ride on a single lane dirt road. It wound around the ocean side of Cape Perpetua and Heceta Head. One minute the road was the beach and the next thing climbing, climbing to 500 feet or more. It hadn't changed much in the past three years. This area was the last truly wild area on the coastal route. Only a couple cars were passed. One of these was the mail carrier high on the steep slope of Perpetua who pulled into the brush to let them pass. "We stopped, of course, to pass the time of day and photograph his truck and our cars. He informed us his truck was geared for 13 forward speeds and 8 in reverse."

The carrier, Si Cooper, made two round trips a week between Yachats and Florence to deliver mail to 40 families and two isolated post offices.

Ten miles later, the road dropped down to the Heceta Head Lighthouse. Then it dropped farther to Cape Creek, crossed a rickety bridge, and climbed a 20-percent grade to Sea Lion Point. No tunnel or nicely paved highway then, and the sea lion caves were not yet a tourist attraction. Also the headland lacked the forest it boasts today. "On this steep headland, we found hundreds of sheep grazing. As we dropped down the south side of the mountain, we had a grand view of the sand dune desert stretching almost to Florence."

The third ferry crossed the Siuslaw River between Florence and Glenada. Then the two cars traveled over a fairly good road to Gardiner, unlike the miserable conditions of the 1926 trip. Then they boarded another ferry for the 2 1/2-mile ride to Reedsport. "The ferryman, A.F. Smith, collected 50 cents a car and assured us that nobody before us had attempted to drive from Astoria to Crescent City in one day. We felt like pioneers."

For the next 32 miles to Coos Bay, the two cars rolled along at good speed over a fine new macadam road, arriving at the free ferry to North Bend in one hour and five minutes. The remainder of the trip passed quickly with a macadam road most of the way. After stopping at Coquille for supper, they arrived about 9 p.m. at Wedderburn where they waited for the ferry. They crossed the Rogue River into Gold Beach about 10 p.m. The only slow section was the winding dirt mountain road between Pistol River and Brookings.

At 12:10 a.m. the Marquette arrived, with the Buick following behind, at the Lauff Hotel in Crescent City — a record 21 hours and 15 minutes from the time they left the Astoria Hotel. Discounting delays, the trip took a little more than 18 hours of driving time. Thus, accomplishing their goal.

Surfing the Coast Highway

Boys climb atop a car foundering in the surf.

Comparing this trip to the 1926 trip demonstrates how quickly improvements were being made on the coast highway. Even so, the 42-mile segment from Waldport to Florence took 4 hours and 10 minutes — an average of 10 miles per hour.

Restricted roads and inconvenient ferries

For the most part, folks living in central coast towns were still restricted to driving roads within town or short distances north and south unless they wanted to brave the beaches or the sometimes-impassable wagon roads. And ferries still played a key part in central coast life.

The ferry in Florence connected to the town of Glenada, which at one time was larger than Florence. Back in 1914, it was an incorporated town with quite a business center, and it was still going strong through the 1920s.

The older "people" ferries were small and Bob Merz, long-time Florence resident, remembers riding one of the not-much-bigger car ferries in the 1920s. "When I was a kid living on a dairy ranch up Fiddle Creek, it used to take the whole day to go to town," he recalled. "We would leave as soon as the milking was done, drive to Glenada, and more often than not have to wait for the ferry. The captain wouldn't depart until the ferry was loaded with its capacity of four cars. My dad would fuss. We often 'wasted' a half hour waiting for the fourth car. It was even worse returning, and my dad fussed all the more. It would be an hour drive to the farm, and the cows would be waiting to be milked."

On May 15, 1932, the state took over the ferry system in Florence and made it free. That's when *Tourist I* began service between Florence and Glenada. Andy Nordahl, who grew up on the river, remembered it well. "The *Tourist I* was the largest of the [Florence] ferries and usually held about 10 cars. The passenger section was behind the pilothouse in the center of the boat, and the cars would park on the outside edge."

The same little girl whose Teddy bear's ears got singed also traveled along the coast in 1932. Derrickson, again going from Tacoma to Los Angeles, accompanied her mother and father and traveled by car. This time, she found the highway considerably improved. One of her favorite memories involved waiting for the ferry to come across from Glenada and the young man by the ferry slip with a boiling pot of crab. "He was selling fresh cooked huge Dungeness crab for 25 cents apiece or five for a dollar. Needless to say, we purchased several, settled for the night in the first 'auto court' we came to, and gorged ourselves on crab."

Jack Saubert, a Florence native, recalls how selling crab at ferry crossings provided him a means of making money when he was a kid. He sold his crab for 10 cents apiece. What a deal!

Fred Jensen, a Florence native from a pioneer family, remembers taking a trip to Marshfield (since 1944 called Coos Bay) in the early 1930s with his dad and granddad to buy some marine supplies. "We went across to Glenada on the ferry, which we boarded about where the gazebo is today. Then when we got to Gardiner, we took another ferry and went upriver to Reedsport," said Jensen. "And the roads were not very straight. They wound around back in the hills. No bridge on Haines Inlet; so we had to go around. Then we crossed Coos Bay on a ferry to North Bend and then on to Marshfield. The road's pretty straight today. But then it was not an easy journey and took all day to get there and back."

Road Crew

An early road crew cuts and fills along a slope near South Beach on the Roosevelt Highway circa 1920s.

CHAPTER 3

~~~~~~

Highway Completed...Almost

Work by Oregon State Highway Department (OSHD) crews began in 1921 on the Roosevelt Highway and continued on year after year. They graded and paved section after section along the 400-mile route that stretched between the Columbia River and the California state line.

Robert W. Hadlow points out in his book *Elegant Arches, Soaring Spans* that in spite of state highway engineer Roy A. Klein repeatedly stating that the coast highway had the highest priority in Oregon's road-building programs, the project dragged on and on. Coast travelers thought it would never end.

Roadway, small bridges, tunnels finished

After a decade of work, the route finally extended the full 400 miles and bridged many of the smaller bodies of water. The road surface, however, was not a continuous stretch of macadam or concrete, and the unpaved sections became muddy when it rained. So packing a shovel was still advisable. And the six remaining ferries still contributed to delays.

Ferries operated on two large bays — Yaquina Bay at Newport

and Coos Bay at North Bend — and four river estuaries — Alsea River at Waldport, Siuslaw River at Florence, Umpqua River at Reedsport, and Rogue River at Gold Beach. Private citizens and coastal chambers of commerce complained bitterly about the slow, unreliable ferry service. So much so that beginning in 1927, the state bridge section started taking over operation of most ferries; they would no longer be private operations. It would be a few years, however, before the state had control of all of them.

Once under state operation, the ferries were free and ran nonstop for 16 hours a day. No more waiting for the ferry to fill up before starting to move; the goal was uninterrupted service. Delays still happened but were due to low water or high water, not to the whims of the ferrymen. And each night the ferries were shut down. In Florence, stranded passengers were allowed to stay in the lobby of the Florence Hotel at no cost.

Most of the small ferries no longer provided service because they had been replaced. Many short-span bridges over streams and small rivers had been constructed right along with the roadwork. Conde B. McCullough, state bridge designer, was respon-

Cape Creek Bridge

The Cape Creek Bridge completed in 1932 is one of McCullough's most intriguing designs with its two-tiered viaduct approach, resembling a Roman aqueduct, particularly the Pont du Gard near Nimes, France. In the upper left is the Heceta Head Lighthouse keeper's house.

sible for many of these smaller bridges and some of them were real gems. According to McCullough scholar Hadlow, "Most notable were a 150-foot deck arch across the mouth of Depoe Bay and a similar structure over Rocky Creek, both in Lincoln County [both completed in 1927]. Each one exhibited features characteristic of his designs."

Another notable deck arch design is the Cape Creek Bridge completed in 1932. It is one of McCullough's most intriguing designs with its two-tiered viaduct approach, resembling a Roman aqueduct, particularly the Pont du Gard near Nimes, France. The bridge is located between Yachats and Florence — one of the last sections of highway to be completed. In this scenic area, towering headlands drop straight into the sea. Not an easy place to build a highway.

Adjacent to the Cape Creek Bridge site, the OSHD crews bored a 700-foot tunnel through Devil's Elbow headland in 1931. Both this tunnel and the one on the north coast at Arch Rock proved extremely difficult. Onno Husing in "A History of U.S. Highway 101," provides this explanation from ODOT geologist Michael Long: "The basalt on the Oregon Coast tends to fracture because millions of years ago, when the lava cooled, it cooled rapidly. That makes these coastal basalt formations more brittle than other basalt formations. With fractured basalt, just imagine how hard it must have been to calibrate how much explosives to use. Workers [in 1931] used a lot of guesswork when they set off dynamite charges." Because of the high cost of constructing the tunnel and Cape Creek Bridge, this section of highway became known as the "million dollar mile."

According to Hadlow, "As early as 1931, Lewis A. McArthur, an Oregon geographer and historian, suggested that state officials change the name of the Roosevelt Coast Military Highway because it misrepresented the route's true function." Within months, it boasted a new name — the Oregon Coast Highway.

By June of the following year, Gold Beach, Marshfield, and Newport, realizing their growth would be retarded due to the inadequate ferries, formed the Oregon Coast Highway Association (OCHA) to continue improvements on the Coast Highway. The group immediately focused on eliminating the ferries and began a push for the last five bridges. Because it represented such a large segment of the coast, OCHA became a major factor in building a coastal identity.

One down, five to go

In 1930, state officials called for constructing a bridge over the Rogue River between Wedderburn and Gold Beach. The Issac Lee Patterson Bridge (named after Oregon's Governor from 1927 to 1929) was completed in late 1931 by Mercer–Fraser Company of Eureka, California. The dedication, however, didn't take place until the following spring. Upon completion, it became the largest Pacific coast bridge between San Francisco and Astoria. It also became the first bridge in the United States to try the Freyssinet method, which allowed lighter, more graceful supports due to the use of less concrete. Although this rather complicated prestressing technique was commonly used in Europe, McCullough wanted to see for himself how it would work in Oregon. As to the design of the 1,898-foot bridge, it incorporated a mix of the aesthetic and the practical — typical McCullough. "He created a multi-arched structure that harmonized with the rolling hills of

I.L. Patterson Bridge

The Issac Lee Patterson Bridge (named after Oregon's Governor from 1927 to 1929) was completed in late 1931 by Mercer–Fraser Company of Eureka, California. Upon completion, it crossed the Rogue River and became the largest Pacific coast bridge between San Francisco and Astoria.

the coastal mountains," wrote Hadlow.

Optimism was in the air with the dedication of the I.L. Patterson Bridge over the Rogue River in April 1932 and continued with the ceremonial opening of the recently renamed Oregon Coast Highway in May, only a month later. The completion of the highway after a decade of work was reason indeed to celebrate. Even though it was considered completed in 1932, sections between Waldport and Gardiner were graded but had not been surfaced yet. It wouldn't be until the summer of 1933 that these last sections would be considered finished.

In spite of these last few unsurfaced sections, the popularity of the scenic coastal route prompted speculation that the state would soon replace ferry service at Newport, Waldport, Florence, Reedsport, and North Bend with structures similar to the

Big Creek Bridge

Big Creek Bridge located between Waldport and Florence is shown under construction and when completed in 1931. This is one of the smaller bridges designed by McCullough along the Coast Highway.

Gold Beach bridge.

Newspapers — both inland and coastal — were rife with proposals, speculation, and rumors. Meanwhile, the ferry situation came to a head.

Ferries and passengers reached limits

A May 1934 article in Florence's *Siuslaw Oar,* titled "Traffic Picking Up on the Coast Highway," printed numbers to show increased ferry usage. January 1933 to '34 increased from 2,888 to 4,095 and April 1933 to '34 increased from 5,393 to 6,997. A record was kept at all ferry crossings of both foot passengers and vehicles. Similar increases were also recorded at the four other coastal ferry crossings.

Tourist I, the last ferry to serve Florence, was 65 feet long and could squeeze in up to 16 cars and 25 passengers when fully loaded, instead of its usual 10-car load. By the end of its runs, *Tourist I* was making 64 15-minute trips a day across the Siuslaw, and the last season averaged 600 cars a day.

Tourist I's 15-minute trips were the shortest of the five ferries. All the others took longer because of larger bays to cross, and between Gardiner and Reedsport, the ferry had to travel about 2 1/2 miles between towns.

After the completion of the highway, numerous rumors spread regarding when and where new bridges would be built. One rumor indicated that the Florence bridge would be the last of the five to be built. Following is an excerpt from a September 1933 editorial from M.D. Morgan, a very understanding *Siuslaw Oar* editor:

That the highway commission is taking a logical view in building the other bridges first must be conceded when one considers the matter from the point of view of service. Ferry service at all the other four points constitutes a real delay to traffic. To speed up this service is quite impossible except at great expense. At Florence, the delay to traffic is negligible.

In September 1934, however, Editor Morgan, took real exception to a report in a Eugene paper when it came to reporting heavy traffic on the ferries on a holiday weekend:

Walter P. Fell, member of the Eugene water board, reported to the Eugene News *that on Labor Day there were strings of cars miles long waiting for ferry service on the coast highway. Mebbe so, mebbe so, Mr. Fell, but not at Florence! The line of waiting cars here at no time exceeded a block and a half or about two ferry loads. The ferry makes a trip in 15 minutes, and this schedule was maintained all day. No one had to wait more than 30 minutes. All records were broken here Sunday when 1,065 cars were shuttled across. Full loads were taken both ways hours at a stretch.*

With "strings of cars miles long waiting for ferry service" and full loads going "both ways hours at a stretch," it sounded like the highway was indeed ready for bridges to replace the five remaining ferry crossings. Both the ferries and their passengers had reached their limits. A report by the state highway commission, with hard numbers showing increased ferry traffic, backed up what visitors to and residents at the coast already knew.

And the building of the I.L. Patterson Bridge over the Rogue River showed that the state had the right designer in Conde B. McCullough to handle large coastal bridges in a way befitting one of the most scenic stretches of highway in the country.

PART II
THE MAN: CONDE B. MCCULLOUGH

~~~~~~

CHAPTER 4

Midwestern Roots

Conde B. McCullough

CONDE B. MCCULLOUGH, born in Redfield, in the Dakota Territory (part of South Dakota today), went on to study civil engineering at Iowa State College (ISC) in Ames between 1906 and 1910. While working toward his degree, he took a variety of courses. McCullough scholar Hadlow noted in an article that "his final semester included a course on the design of stone, brick, and reinforced-concrete arches." This would turn out to be one of his most useful courses. He graduated with a Bachelor of Science degree in civil engineering in 1910.

Marston's influence

While at ISC, McCullough came under the tutelage of faculty member Anson Marston, one of the nation's leading engineers. According to *Oregon Stater* editor George P. Edmonston Jr. in an article about McCullough's bridges, "Marston told his students they must be able to do more than crunch numbers and supervise workers. Instead, the old dean pushed for the 'well-rounded' engineer, a professional with a respect for the past and an eye for the aesthetic." This greatly influenced the young engineer.

Marsh's rainbow arch

After graduation, McCullough took a job with James Marsh, owner of the Marsh Engineering Company in Des Moines, Iowa. Marsh specialized in reinforced concrete bridges and had patented a "rainbow arch" design, which had been incorporated into numerous public works bridges throughout more than one Midwestern state. "In this design," Hadlow wrote, "Marsh used steel plating and concrete to construct the road deck and through-arch system, instead of the traditional steel-truss spans, and Marsh believed that he could produce it at comparable cost. Marsh promoted his bridge as frost-proof, flood-proof, and fireproof — a permanent structure that required little maintenance. Marsh greatly influenced the development of McCullough's philosophy of bridge design, one that the younger man would espouse for the next 35 years."

Although McCullough stayed with Marsh for only a year, he not only learned about bridge design but also about the fierce competition between private companies to win bridge-building contracts from county governments.

ISHC's continuing education

In 1911, Marston reentered McCullough's life and persuaded him to join the Iowa State Highway Commission (ISHC), which had been located at Iowa State College since its inception in 1904. During the ISHC's first seven years, there was only one employee — Thomas H. MacDonald — and the commission was limited to offering only technical advice on road construction to Iowa's counties. In 1911, McCullough's hiring doubled the size of the commission. As assistant engineer, he got busy drafting plans for small bridges and culverts for county use.

During this time in Iowa, some corrupt and incompetent construction companies were building substandard bridges, roads, and culverts, with taxpayer money. According to Onno Husing, director of Oregon Coastal Zone Management Association (OCZMA), writing about McCullough, "Things got so bad that in 1913, the Iowa legislature required counties to follow road and bridge designs prepared by the ISHC. This mandate on local government made Iowa a national leader in highway development."

It also allowed the ISHC to expand and reorganize. McCullough became a member of a group of college graduates serving under MacDonald. During this period, he learned that having a thorough understanding of the state's topography was very important, and that many factors needed to be considered in order to select an appropriate bridge type for each site. For starters, on stream, river, and bay crossings, he would need to know stream behavior and navigational requirements for the site.

When it came to traffic use, he would have to consider sight distance, movement and density of vehicles, and future traffic needs. And he also learned to consider the route of the road on either end in relation to siting the bridge.

He believed that "architectural features and scenic considerations," as he referred to them, be seriously considered when selecting a bridge type. This is one area in which he stood out; for many bridge builders, these factors were not even considered.

And, finally, the bottom line! McCullough never forgot that he was working with taxpayers' money and didn't want to waste it. So the choice of bridge type could hinge on construction versus maintenance costs. McCullough found that bridges made of concrete and steel usually had higher construction costs but lower maintenance costs. He came to believe that the less expensive timber bridges became quite expensive to maintain and didn't last as long, and these factors made them more expensive in the long run.

During his years working with the state in Iowa, McCullough turned each bridge designing and building experience into a learning experience and in so doing became a master bridge designer — making each bridge fit its own site.

Luten's lawsuit

One of McCullough's greatest learning experiences involved a lawsuit. It also became one of his biggest challenges. In 1914, his job required him to gather evidence regarding litigation in a patent infringement case. According to Hadlow, "The case originated in 1900 when Daniel B. Luten, founder and president of the Luten Engineering Company and the National Bridge Company, began patenting many components of reinforced-concrete arch bridges. . . . Luten customarily received a 10 percent royalty fee from bridge contracts that employed his patented design components. . . . Luten filed suit in federal court in 1912 against the Marsh Engineering Company of Des Moines, Iowa, alleging that James Marsh had illegally used Luten's designs in a reinforced-concrete arch bridge at Albert Lea, Minnesota, about one hundred miles from Ames."

The ISHC studied Luten's charges against Marsh, McCullough's former boss and a respected bridge designer the state used as a consultant, and concluded that Luten interpreted his patent too broadly and was making a royalties grab at taxpayers' expense. The ISHC decided to fight back, which caused McCullough and his staff additional work during the next three years. Because this was one of 11 similar pending cases nationwide involving Luten, it held special significance. With the assistance of legal counsel, McCullough traced the international development of reinforced bridge construction before 1900. He even went back as far as the Romans, trying to cast doubt on Luten's claims to originality of design.

According to Hadlow, "The work of McCullough and his staff included 600 pages of printed testimony and 150 exhibits, of which 15 were bridge models. . . . The case was a milestone in American civil engineering. The court declared virtually all of Luten's patents invalid and censured him for his unethical business practices. *Luten v Marsh Engineering Company* led to similar verdicts involving bridge engineering patents in Kansas, Oklahoma, and Nebraska."

By compiling a persuasive body of evidence that would win the lawsuit for his old employer, McCullough acquired enough in-depth knowledge about the capabilities of concrete to serve him for a lifetime. And he became aware of what was happening with reinforced concrete in the rest of the world.

Iowa's loss, Oregon's gain

McCullough, constantly on a quest to find efficient and economical solutions to engineering problems, found that at that time, there wasn't much professional literature available. Consequently, he spent long hours on basic and applied research. He became known as an authority on bridge engineering partly due to his research and partly due to his excellent mathematical skills in engineering calculations. Because of his expertise, he often provided expert testimony in court cases against unscrupulous bridge companies. Through these experiences, he earned professional recognition throughout the country.

He and the team of college graduates he worked with created several plans for reinforced-concrete bridges and culverts that were widely adopted. According to Hadlow, it wasn't long before federal engineers praised the standardization program that McCullough created. They commented that Iowa had "the best bridges and culverts of any state in the Union."

With his growing national reputation, McCullough received an invitation from Oregon to teach structural engineering at Oregon Agricultural College (today's Oregon State University). To McCullough, Oregon was a place of varied topography offering a multitude of streams and rivers, ravines and canyons to cross. To this emerging master of bridge design, he couldn't resist.

Great Place to Walk

The walkway along a tied arch on the Siuslaw River Bridge. Note one of the bridge's distinctive pier houses in the distance.

CHAPTER 5

~~~~~

Oregon Educator / Bridge Builder

NOT ONLY was there a great need for bridges when McCullough arrived on the scene in Oregon, but roads too were in short supply. Within a few years, the state realized just how useful McCullough could be in fulfilling these needs.

Throughout his career in Oregon, McCullough found it very beneficial to maintain contact between the college — where he taught — and the state bridge section — where he had a decades-long career. He also stayed in touch with colleagues in Iowa. These contacts, both within the state and beyond, helped make his amazing accomplishments possible.

Teaching college

In 1916 with his Iowa education and experience, he moved to Corvallis with his wife, Marie, and their infant son, John, to accept a teaching and research position as assistant professor of civil engineering at Oregon Agricultural College (OAC).

He began his college teaching career as the sole faculty member of the school's structural engineering program within the civil engineering department. The whole department numbered only four faculty members before McCullough.

McCullough taught senior courses to students in the civil engineering program specializing in structural engineering, and he also taught upper-division courses to highway engineering undergraduates. By 1917, McCullough was promoted to professor of civil engineering.

During his teaching years, he also participated in part-time consulting work with the newly organized Oregon State Highway Commission (OSHC). There he established a friendship with Charles Purcell, Oregon's first state bridge engineer, who had moved on to become a design engineer for Multnomah County.

Although, McCullough remained a faculty member at OAC for only three years, he did return to teach night classes in the late 1920s and maintained ties with the civil engineering department for decades. He remained a teacher, however, throughout his life, educating the public and those he worked with on his views that bridges should be economical, structurally sound, and aesthetically pleasing.

Building bridges

In 1919, when Oregon became the first state in the nation

Conde B. McCullough at work in his office.

to establish a fuel tax of 1 cent a gallon as a source of income for highway construction and maintenance, it, of course, included bridges. Since Purcell's departure in 1915, the position of state bridge engineer had been vacant. But with increased funding, more engineers and draftsmen would be needed. Herbert Nunn, recently appointed state highway engineer, offered McCullough the position of state bridge engineer in the spring of 1919. McCullough readily accepted and moved his family to Salem.

"His first responsibility was to hire a staff," wrote George Edmonston, "and for this he chose the entire graduating class in civil engineering at Oregon State, all five of them, of whom four accepted: Ellsworth G. Ricketts, Raymond "Peany" Archibald, Mervyn "Steve" Stephenson, and Albert G. Skelton." OAC officials gave approval, as long as the students completed their remaining course work and returned for graduation. McCullough assigned them to district offices where they gained practical experience on a variety of projects.

Edmonston also wrote that "OAC students worshipped McCullough, always hoping to be the next Oregon Stater he would hire."

McCullough also convinced some of his former classmates from Iowa to come to Oregon. Surrounding himself with former students from OAC and classmates from Iowa, he formed a close-knit organization of professionals. As McCullough assembled this team of bridge designers and resident engineers, his old boss from Iowa, Thomas H. MacDonald, was appointed by President Woodrow Wilson to be the next director of the U.S. Bureau of Public Roads (BPR). Talk about having friends in high places!

In his role as director of the bridge-building section, McCullough excelled. The low-cost, custom-designed structures the department designed and built were characterized by architectural elegance. By the end of fiscal year 1920, the department under McCullough had been responsible for 162 new bridges. Most were short reinforced-concrete deck girder spans, but a few were reinforced-concrete arches.

The reinforced-concrete arch was McCullough's first choice for many bridge designs, and when the roadway approaches made it possible, he liked to create side views of a bridge's arches and spandrel columns so the motorists could have a better appreciation of what they would be traveling over.

And he also cared about close-up views. "By the mid-1920s, McCullough increasingly incorporated classical details into his reinforced-concrete spans," explained Hadlow. "He designed Gothic-arched panels to support beveled handrails and added decorative brackets below the outer edges of the road deck. These components were relatively inexpensive because they were precast during construction and assembled at the site."

In a period of six years, McCullough and his section designed and built almost 600 bridges throughout Oregon. Because each bridge's design fit its location, each blended in with the natural setting. As the 1920s progressed, the section designed and built fewer but larger bridges.

Hadlow summed up Oregon's impressive state bridge engineer best: "McCullough designed efficient, economical, and elegant stream crossings. He was an original thinker with superior mathematical abilities, an eye for design, a great knowledge of bridge building worldwide, and efficient managerial skills. Like nineteenth-century engineering figures — McCullough combined an engineer's desire for creating efficient structures with public funds and an architect's drive for aesthetic excellence."

Ten Mile Creek Bridge

The Ten Mile Creek Bridge is one of three almost identical tied-arch bridges McCullough designed to span difficult locations.

CHAPTER 6

~~~~~

Innovative Designer of Masterpieces

For McCullough, the years from 1925 to 1932 represented a period where he added additional hats. He continued on as the state bridge engineer but also became an author and a lawyer and took on complex challenges. As an author, he promoted the economics of bridge building through a textbook written for engineering students and for those working in the field — *Economics of Highway Bridge Types*. This was the first of many books and shorter publications he was to write over the years.

In 1925, he went back to school for three years to earn his law degree because of his abiding interest in litigation as it pertained to road and bridge building. He worked his day-job around his law school classes and received his law degree in 1928 from Willamette University's School of Law. Shortly after that, he was admitted to the Oregon Bar. And his willingness to not back away from challenges, no matter how difficult, prompted him to investigate unusual design and construction techniques. The knowledge he gained and shared during these years contributed to the greater knowledge of bridge engineering both in principle and in practice.

Engineering innovations

"While he had an affinity for the reinforced-concrete arch, he never lost sight of the need for greater understanding of other bridge types and cultivated a personal interest in movable span bridges — bascule spans, swing spans, and vertical lift spans," wrote Hadlow. "He designed two bascule drawbridges [Old Youngs Bay and Lewis and Clark River bridges] for the northernmost portion of the Roosevelt Coast Military Highway in 1920, and consulted on reconstruction of Portland's many movable structures spanning the Willamette River." This background came in handy when he designed two more movable spans along the coast in 1936 — one in Florence and one in Reedsport.

Among the most challenging bridges on the coast highway were three similar small stream crossings designed in 1931: the Wilson River in the Tillamook area and Big Creek and Ten Mile Creek on the central coast. According to Hadlow: "Their 100-foot-wide channels, with sandy foundations, prevented McCullough from using traditional arches, which required abutment piers to counter lateral thrust. The high water level of all

Cape Creek Bridge Under Construction

The highway at Cape Creek will pass high over the creek and then through a 700-foot tunnel bored into Devil's Elbow headland. This section became known as the "million dollar mile."

three streams was close to roadway grades, which ruled out alternative reinforced-concrete, deck-girder spans. Finally, the harsh coastal environment, with its corrosive salt air, precluded the use of steel-truss spans. Accordingly, McCullough created identical 120-foot [reinforced-concrete] tied arches for all three crossings. They were some of the first bridges of this type in the United States and were the first in the Far West."

Similar problems occurred with other small coastal bridges. Twelve miles north of Florence, OSHD wanted to realign the road at Cape Creek by passing high over the stream's deep canyon and tunneling 700 feet through Devil's Elbow headland before heading south along this winding stretch of coast. This was the previously mentioned "million-dollar mile." "McCullough looked at many possible design alternatives before deciding to build a bridge consisting of a reinforced-concrete arch with two-tiered viaduct approaches," wrote Hadlow. . . . "The structure's vertical support members dispersed its load on the unstable foundations, and cross bracing between the piers and panels prevented lateral movement. . . . The Cape Creek Bridge [completed in 1932] was McCullough's and Oregon's only Roman-style concrete viaduct."

Under President Herbert Hoover's administration, there was a modest public works program. McCullough tapped into it by partnering with the Bureau of Public Roads (BPR), headed by MacDonald. As a result, the federal government paid for two thirds of the cost of the Cape Creek Bridge. And a few miles north of Cape Creek, McCullough also partnered with the BPR in 1931 to build a bridge across Cummins Creek, which was also part of the Oregon Coast Highway.

The Isaac Lee Patterson Bridge at Gold Beach over the Rogue River was the first structure completed in the United States using French engineer Eugene Freyssinet's methods for reinforced-concrete arch rib pre-compression. According to Freyssinet, this method made construction possible of more graceful looking large-scale arches due to using more slender ribs. McCullough saw this technique as one that might reduce construction costs, thus saving public funds.

McCullough tried the Freyssinet method as part of an experiment in bridge design — again in partnership with the BPR. It became a field study to test the advantages and disadvantages. And a group of young Oregon State Agricultural College (OSAC, the word "state" was added in 1927) graduates assisted in gathering data during construction. Two years later, McCullough and Albin L. Gemeny, senior structural engineer with the test division of the BPR, produced a 60-page report documenting their conclusions. Although the Freyssinet method did use less reinforcing bar and concrete, it required additional skilled labor, which proved in the end just as expensive as more traditional construction. McCullough never used the Freyssinet method again.

Because the I.L. Patterson Bridge was one of the first uses of pre-stressed concrete bridge construction in the United States, what McCullough learned added to the annals of bridge building. In 1982, the bridge was designated a National Historic Civil Engineering Landmark by the American Society of Civil Engineers. According to Hadlow, "Freyssinet went on to perfect pre-stressed concrete beam bridge construction that became commonplace on the nation's roads after World War II."

Engineering Innovations

Considére hinges make bridges like the Yaquina Bay Bridge possible because they allow long span arches on concrete piers supported by timber piling foundations.

The Freyssinet method wasn't the only European technique McCullough tried. He tried the Considére hinge, developed by Armand Considére. It is a short cushioning block of heavily reinforced concrete with a relatively small cross-section, which made it possible to support long span arches on piers supported by timber piling foundations. This was a technique that became a part of his bridge building repertoire; he used it again and again.

Besides trying the techniques of two Frenchmen, McCullough was greatly influenced by the Swiss master of the reinforced-concrete bridge, Robert Maillart (1872–1940), who rejected rigidity of form. A bridge designer of international stature, he was known for graceful reinforced-concrete spans that seemed to float over deep mountain chasms that they spanned. McCullough was very impressed with the way Maillart's bridges didn't dominate, but seemed to grow out of the landscape and united economy, function, and beauty. Here was a bridge designer he could really relate to.

Designing masterpieces

McCullough's large-span designs throughout Oregon launched him into national and international prominence. Hadlow explains, "McCullough's five large-span bridges at Newport, Waldport, Florence, Reedsport, and North Bend represented the pinnacle of bridge design for their use of engineering advances and their architectural style to fit the natural setting. Critics both contemporary and later on saw them as masterpieces in design."

For McCullough they also represented his "pinnacle of design, both aesthetically and technically." Hadlow goes on to say, "More than his previous structures, this group of bridges featured the possibilities of reinforced concrete. Because of the plasticity of this medium, designers like McCullough could cast concrete with any desired form, not necessarily mimicking masonry construction."

On these five coastal bridges, McCullough continued using techniques whose success had been demonstrated in earlier projects. The vibrating machines that rid freshly poured concrete of air pockets and made it firmer and more uniform is a good example.

Just as techniques evolved, his designs evolved with influences from various sources. The classic Roman arch, however, remained a constant in his designs.

"In 1933 when McCullough designed the five major coastal bridges, he took a dramatic turn to Gothic architecture," said Onno Husing, Director of OCZMA. "McCullough, like the stonemasons who built the Gothic cathedrals, used pointed arches as well as the classic rounded arches in these iconic bridge structures." While he had some Gothic influences in his work previously, more were included in the five coastal bridges.

Husing is convinced that the St. Johns Bridge in Portland, which was completed in 1931, influenced McCullough. Husing explains, "In 1929, Multnomah County commissioned the building of the St. Johns Bridge across the Willamette River. An open national design competition was held. One of America's leading bridge designers, David B. Steinman (1886–1960) from New York City entered and won. Steinman, who grew up in the shadow of the Brooklyn Bridge, submitted an uncommonly beautiful Gothic steel suspension bridge design. McCullough entered the design competition, but, like the others, he lost out to Steinman.

However, because of the competition, Steinman and McCullough became good friends."

Within a couple of years, McCullough was incorporating more Gothic themes into viaducts, balustrades, and other components of his bridges. At the Yaquina Bay and Coos Bay bridges, towering Gothic arches became the main support piers. On the Siuslaw River and Umpqua River bridges, Gothic arches support the viaducts. And driving through the cantilevered structure on the Coos Bay Bridge is driving through Gothic arch after Gothic arch.

And, finally, the five coastal bridges incorporated an amazing array of Art Deco and other decorative motifs that became a McCullough trademark. He decorated pylons, obelisks, piers, and other flat surfaces. According to Husing, "Poured concrete proved to be an ideal medium for Art Deco. Despite seasonally high winds and exposure to salt air,

Master bridge builder
Conde B. McCullough

295
7-23-36
1/23

Coos Bay Bridge

The mile-long Coos Bay Bridge with the double cantilever over the navigation channel was an engineering marvel.

the concrete work remains remarkably intact."

The six major bridges that McCullough designed and built for the coast during the first half of the 1930s represented a culmination of years of studying and designing. On June 4, 1934, during a period of time between the designing and building of the five bridges of the Coast Bridges Project, McCullough was presented with an Honorary Doctorate of Engineering degree at OSAC. This degree recognized McCullough for his contributions to the state of Oregon as well as to the entire field of bridge engineering.

Getting those five bridges built during the dark days of the Depression was to become a monumental task. Even though the ferries had reached their limits, people were clamoring for the bridges, and McCullough and the bridge section were ready with one bridge already under design, the state just didn't have the money. Any hope lay with the federal government.

A Master of Arts

The five coastal bridges incorporated an amazing array of Art Deco and other decorative motifs that became a McCullough trademark, as displayed here in the Siuslaw River Bridge's tied arch and pier house. He decorated pylons, obelisks, piers, and other flat surfaces. According to Onno Husing, "Poured concrete proved to be an ideal medium for Art Deco. Despite seasonally high winds and exposure to salt air, the concrete work remains remarkably intact."

PART III
THE TIME: ROOSEVELT'S NEW DEAL

~~~~

CHAPTER 7
Potential Federal Support

THE STATE DECLARED the Oregon Coast Highway officially completed in April 1932, although, five major rivers and bays did not yet have bridges. Having a highway that stretched the whole 400-mile length of the state was a boon to the individual communities, the coastal region, and the state. Traffic dramatically increased. With the heavier traffic, however, it quickly became apparent that the five remaining ferries were inadequate. "The State Highway Commission called them a 'barrier to the growth and development of the Oregon coast region,'" wrote historian Gary Link.

The state considered constructing one bridge each year even before the completion of the highway in 1932. And after the I.L. Patterson Bridge in Gold Beach was completed in late 1931, the increasingly powerful Oregon Coast Highway Association (OCHA) pressured the Oregon State Highway Commission (OSHC) to construct another bridge right away. But the state didn't have the money for another such undertaking; since 1929, the Depression had drained the state's resources. OSHC felt that it wouldn't be any use in trying to sell bonds to raise money for the bridges, in spite of overwhelming public support. As a last resort, Oregonians looked to the Hoover Administration for help.

HOOVER'S RFC

According to Hadlow, "In the late summer of 1932, Oregonians sought federal help. Congress had recently approved the Relief and Construction Act, which, in part, set aside $120 million in loans for state road construction and maintenance. The lawmakers also created the Reconstruction Finance Corporation (RFC) to loan funds to states for toll bridges and other large-scale projects requiring long-term repayment schedules." The OCHA continued to be in the forefront of the battle to build bridges over the five remaining ferry crossings. So they petitioned the Oregon State Highway Department (OSHD) to apply for RFC loans for this purpose. Coastal chambers of commerce endorsed the plan because it called for wooden bridges. Naturally, they had high hopes of locally harvested timber cut in local mills.

"McCullough endorsed the Coast Highway Association's general plan for replacing the five ferry crossings with bridges," wrote Hadlow. "A toll of twenty-five cents per vehicle spread over six to ten years, McCullough believed, would generate the $3 million necessary for bridge construction costs." Possible RFC funding raised hopes for new bridges, but not for long. In September 1932, the RFC declared the proposal ineligible for funding because it violated RFC's guidelines for self-supporting projects. The repayment plan included money from gasoline and vehicle license fees. However, by November this was a moot point because of the election of President Franklin Roosevelt. The new administration came into office with new plans, and the RFC would soon be cancelled.

Roosevelt's PWA

On Saturday, March 4, 1933, President Roosevelt delivered his famous inaugural address from the steps of the U.S. Capitol. FDR declared to a stricken nation, "This Nation asks for action, and action now!" Husing, who was impressed with the speed in which things happened under Roosevelt, says, "Seventeen days later, President Roosevelt sent a message to Congress calling for the establishment of an ambitious public works relief program to rescue the economy."

This public works program would be larger than that of the previous administration and would try to provide jobs to unemployed Americans through the construction of public roads, dams, buildings, and bridges. "Charles L. McNary, a Republican from Oregon, became U.S. Senate minority leader in March of 1933 and helped spearhead a bipartisan campaign supporting Franklin Roosevelt's New Deal programs," wrote Hadlow. "He

wholeheartedly lobbied for legislation that created the National Recovery Administration and the Public Works Administration (PWA)." Expectations were high for imminent approval of this public works legislation, which was expected to distribute $2 to $3 billion. And it wasn't long before this legislation received approval.

By May 1933, OSHD began preparing the applications for financial assistance from the soon-to-be-created PWA. "The department asked for a 30 percent outright grant and a 70 percent loan of the estimated $3.4 million in construction costs for five new coastal bridges," wrote Hadlow. "Because of the projects' labor-intensive nature, Devers [Joseph M. Devers, legal counsel for the OSHD] and McCullough believed that the proposal was appropriate for PWA funding. They estimated it would employ 750 workers for up to two years and that it would create an additional 375 jobs, supplying materials to the construction sites."

Congressional approval would be needed because some of the five proposed bridges would be over shipping channels that were under War Department jurisdiction. So OSHC requested McNary's help. By May 11, he had introduced five nearly identical bills authorizing Oregon to "construct, maintain, and operate" the proposed bridges and by June 12, President Roosevelt signed them into law. The bridges weren't a done deal yet; the War Department needed to approve the designs and Congress needed to approve funding.

McCullough's mad scramble

Suddenly, it was all happening too fast. Four of the five bridge designs were not even begun yet. "State bridge engineer McCullough explained, 'When the opportunity of securing federal

Five Proposed Bridges

These are the sketches McCullough unveiled to the public October 1933. Top: Yaquina Bay and Alsea Bay bridges. Middle: Siuslaw River and Umpqua River bridges. Bottom: Coos Bay Bridge.

financing for the structures arose, no planning on any bridges except for the Alsea Bay Bridge at Waldport had been done,'" wrote historian Gary Link.

With high hopes that design approval and federal financing would come through, McCullough doubled the size of his staff. He brought some of the more experienced district engineers to Salem and recruited others, including more from OSAC. He split this expanded team into day and night shifts, 6 a.m. to 3 p.m. and 3 p.m. to midnight, because there were not enough tables for all of them to work at the same time. The designers and engineers had to work at top speed to complete the remaining four bridge drawings between June and September.

McCullough was confident enough to inform the press in early June that his plans were far enough along to allow him to begin building the Alsea Bay Bridge at Waldport within 30 days of funding. And he added that he could contract construction for the other four spans by the end of summer, pending funding. His fingers might have been crossed behind his back on that last statement.

McCullough's bridge designers and engineers deferred to McCullough's expertise and intimate involvement in designing each bridge. This interview by Louis F. Pierce with Ivan Merchant [OAC class of 1929] as quoted in Hadlow's *Elegant Arches, Soaring Spans* describes how McCullough worked: "Mac would lay out the overall job," Merchant recalled. "He would pick up a piece of paper and a pencil and say, 'Now . . . this is about what you are going to do.' . . . And about every two or three weeks, he'd come back to see how you were getting along."

Meanwhile, McCullough spent time at each of the five bridge sites, taking into consideration all of the factors necessary for a bridge to function adequately, to be an economical use of the taxpayers' money, and to make use of all the new bridge building techniques he had pioneered and determined to be useful during his past two decades as a bridge builder. Besides the functionality, economics, and new technology, he also made sure that the bridges were pleasing to the eye and blended well with their locations. Consequently, McCullough made numerous trips back and forth.

By August 1933, the double shifts of designers had completed plans for bridges over Alsea Bay and the Siuslaw River. The Umpqua River Bridge design was expected by mid-August and the Coos Bay and Yaquina Bay bridges' designs by October 1. OSHD submitted its plans to the Oregon office of the PWA in Portland in mid-September, two weeks ahead of the schedule set in June. Because of higher materials and labor costs, estimates had risen to $5.1 million.

Meanwhile, coastal communities did not know what was happening, and newspaper articles speculated endlessly. So in early October 1933, McCullough unveiled sketches of the proposed bridges to let them know what was planned.

What was actually happening were important exchanges between Salem and Portland: "Between October 1933 and April 1934 in the Portland PWA office," wrote Hadlow, "field engineers from the BPR were busily inspecting hundreds of sheets of construction drawings and work schedules that McCullough and his designers had finished in September. Many of the plans were passed back and forth between Salem's bridge department and the federal offices in Portland until both sides agreed that they met criteria established by the American Association of

State Highway Officials (AASHO), the War Department, and the PWA."

For the bridge over Yaquina Bay at Newport, the bridge section designed a 3,223-foot bridge consisting of a series of reinforced-concrete deck arches (below the road deck), with a 600-foot steel through arch (that cars drive through) flanked by a pair of steel deck arches (below the road deck). For Waldport, they designed a 3,011-foot bridge that included reinforced-concrete deck girder and deck-arch approaches (below the road deck) to three reinforced-concrete through tied arches (that cars drive through) over Alsea Bay's navigation channel. This bridge was the only one to be built totally of reinforced-concrete with no steel sections.

Because both the Siuslaw and Umpqua rivers supported shipping traffic and the sites were not high or wide enough to provide a high clearance, movable spans were required that could accommodate taller vessels. The designs featured bridges with movable center spans. At Florence for the Siuslaw's deep narrow channel, the bridge section designed a 1,568-foot structure featuring deck-girder approaches with a central section of two reinforced-concrete tied arches (that cars drive through) on either side of a double-leaf bascule lift span. At Reedsport for the Umpqua's wide but shallow shipping channel, they designed a 2,206-foot bridge with a steel tied-arch swing span flanked by pairs of reinforced concrete tied arches (all of which cars drive through).

Finally, at North Bend over Coos Bay, the bridge section designed a 5,305-foot bridge with a series of reinforced concrete deck-arch approaches (below the road deck) on both sides leading to a central trussed-steel cantilever section measuring 1,708 feet long (that cars drive through). With a wide bay and a need for high clearance, cantilever construction made sense. It would also solve the problem of how to build a bridge without blocking the shipping channel with temporary work bridges during construction.

Between June and the first of October when the last plans were submitted, McCullough and the bridge section really had to scramble, but they persevered and accomplished what they set out to do. The results were plans for five bridges with which everyone could be pleased. . . . Well, almost everyone!

Cathedral Arches

The cathedral-like quality is readily apparent in this view below the Siuslaw River Bridge.

Wood vs Concrete and Steel

Small logging operations that were struggling during the Depression wanted the coastal bridges to be built of wood.

CHAPTER 8

~~~

Timber vs Concrete & Steel

JUST LIKE TODAY, whenever federal funds are being spent, politics, controversy, and delays are part of the process. Because of the Depression, some were against spending money on anything. Others pushed for wooden bridges to help those employed in the timber industry.

Building the five bridges of wood sounded good to the Oregon Coast Highway Association. On June 30, 1932, the group met and former Governor Norblad spoke and proposed building three bridges as a means to create a market for lumber production in the coastal areas. So when McCullough unveiled the sketches of the five proposed concrete and steel bridges in the fall of 1933, controversy arose almost immediately.

The Depression had hit the timber industry especially hard. With 90 percent of companies nearly bankrupt, bridges built of treated wood would have been a great shot in the arm. The Northwest in the early 1930s existed in a state of economic collapse, especially Oregon with half or more of its timberlands tax delinquent. None of the proposals for the new bridges called for wood construction. Therefore, it was no surprise that locals objected to building bridges out of steel and concrete when lumber was plentiful and inexpensive and the timber industry in dire need.

"McCullough listened but wasn't buying. The harsh weather of the coast was his objection," wrote Edmonston. "Wood structures would have to be constantly maintained and their stability over an extended period of time could not be trusted. Concrete and steel were needed, and he pushed this fact everywhere he went." Consequently, his views received criticism all along the coast.

OSHC considered timber bridges, but decided they would not work because of high maintenance costs due to the damp climate, high winds, and salt air. And they felt a few of the spans would be too long for successful wooden bridges. Also, OSHC preferred the bridges be constructed of steel and concrete, because they would last much longer. State officials also argued that the amount of wood required for the falsework and forms for the concrete in the construction of concrete and steel bridges would use almost as much wood as if the bridges themselves were made of wood. Still, lumber interests weren't buying any of these arguments.

"At a highway commission meeting in Portland they pushed for the use of wood on the coastal bridges. McCullough feared that if their pressure caused delay, the federal money would go elsewhere," wrote Link. Further delays over the timber issue raised these same fears among coastal chambers of commerce. And it wasn't long before they voted to support the state in its plan for concrete and steel bridges. Eventually, more of the public came around.

In the end, McCullough got his way, especially "when it was revealed that the War Department's Corps of Engineers would not approve plans for large-span bridges constructed of wood over navigable waters," wrote Hadlow.

From late 1933 into 1934, McCullough championed the construction of the five bridges wherever he went. He received numerous invitations to speak at luncheons and dinners, and he happily accepted them all. According to Hadlow, "At one such engagement at North Bend, *The Coos Bay Times* quoted him as saying that the 400-mile coast highway was the 'finest major route in the world.' When asked about his proposed bridges, he pictured them not merely as structures carrying traffic, but as 'jeweled clasps in a wonderful string of matched pearls.' "

When asked about his proposed bridges, McCullough said he pictured them not merely as structures carrying traffic, but as "jeweled clasps in a wonderful string of matched pearls."

The Siuslaw River Bridge

CHAPTER 9

~~~~

Federal Funding

ON JANUARY 6, 1934, the PWA approved the financial package to build the five coastal bridges to replace the remaining ferries. The agreement made it official that the state would receive 30 percent as an outright grant and 70 percent as a loan secured through bonds. McCullough's "jeweled clasps" would indeed become a reality.

A few days later on the 12th, the headline in Florence's *Siuslaw Oar* declared triumphantly, "Five Coast Bridges Get O.K. by P.W.A." Editor M.D. Morgan went on to say, "First information of the approval of the Siuslaw Bridge by Public Works Administration was received in Florence last Saturday by a telegram to *The Siuslaw Oar* from Congressman James W. Mott. Other messages began to arrive and the local telephone office was kept busy in assisting to spread the glad news over the countryside."

Similar reactions reverberated all along the coast. At long last, the coast highway — all 400 miles of it — would be connected and would, finally, become a *real* highway. And there would be jobs — lots of jobs! This was, indeed, good news.

The only not-so-good news was that bonds would be secured by tolls, which were very unpopular. Some coastal communities harbored the fear that tolls might hinder the California tourist trade. Other Oregonians, living far from the coast, felt that automobile owners throughout the state should not be required to help finance the coast's bridges. Wisely, the PWA turned the issue over to Oregon's lawmakers. It would be awhile before this controversy was settled.

The *Oar* article continued, "Workers will be selected from unemployed men registered at federal bureaus. Men from the counties in which the bridges are located will be given first choice until all capable workers on the unemployed lists are exhausted." The PWA had its own administrative staff, but private contractors did the construction work. They were urged — but not required — to hire the unemployed.

John Fiedler, writing in the *Siuslaw News* when the bridge turned 65 years old, recounted the experiences of a couple of local men when they applied to work on the building of the bridge. They were asked what their occupations had been, and both said farmers and fishermen. They were told that they were the

Masters of Stonework

CCC crew members included expert stone masons who left their mark on (clockwise from top) the bath house on the shores of Cleawox Lake, the West Shelter near the top of Cape Perpetua, a stone mail box at the park ranger's residence at Honeyman State Park. Inset photo tells the story of Oliver "Bud" Hinshaw who worked on the Cape Perpetua shelter.

Cape Perpetua Scenic Area

More Mud, Bud!

For Oliver "Bud" Hinshaw, the West Shelter meant a Civilian Conservation Corps construction job. In 1934, Bud and a crew of five other men put muscle to rock, giving shape to the shelter that has been bracing the Cape Perpetua elements ever since.

Bud's job was keeping the crew supplied with mortar—called *mud*—for the stonework. He also made coffee for the crew—he'd just dump ground coffee and water in a 3½ gallon bucket and bring it to a boil.

The crew built the shelter during the winter. Sometimes it would storm so hard they'd have to huddle in a lean-to where a fire and Bud's coffee kept them warm until conditions improved.

"I don't think the project was so hard," Bud said. "It was just a matter of having patience. That's one thing I have."

best kind to work on a bridge because they were used to looking where they stepped! . . . Good skill to have on a bridge.

It was the Depression and the New Deal was in place with its goal to get people to work through putting out "big bucks for big jobs" through the PWA, Civilian Conservation Corps (CCC), the Rural Electrification Administration (REA), and the Works Progress Administration (WPA renamed Work Projects Administration in 1939). Some references refer to the five bridges being built by the WPA, but that is not exactly correct. Funding for the five bridges came through the PWA, which was supervised by the WPA. And private contractors that bid for the jobs hired the workers who did the actual building. As is often the case when dealing with the government, it was complicated.

Besides the Siuslaw River Bridge, the Florence area benefited through the CCC building Honeyman State Park and the REA bringing electricity to town.

When the late Goodren Gallo, a long-time Florence resident, was in her 90s, she remembered back to when her future husband, Carmine, worked for the CCC on the coast. "As soon as President Roosevelt took office in March 1933 (wasn't January back then), he had the CCCs up and running in no time, planting

West Shelter

A rock wall leads to the West Shelter on a bluff at Cape Perpetua.

trees and working in parks. My husband put in his two years [the limit] under one name and because his mother remarried, changed his name and was able to sign up for another two years. Then he did contract work for the CCCs for two more years. He was involved with building the highway and the parks — Muriel Ponsler Wayside and Honeyman. Stonework was what he enjoyed the most."

The CCC contributed beautiful stonework at a number of places along the coast highway, including at Neahkahnie Mountain on the north coast and at Cape Perpetua and the Heceta Head/Sea Lion Caves area on the central coast. This stonework is still doing its job and is still a work of art.

According to *America Builds: The Record of the PWA* as quoted in *Wikipedia. org,* "More than any other New Deal program, the PWA epitomized the Rooseveltian notion of 'priming the pump' to encourage economic growth. Between July 1933 and March 1939, the PWA funded and administered the construction of more than 34,000 projects including airports, large electricity generating dams, major warships for the Navy, and bridges, as well as 70 percent of new schools and one third of new hospitals built between 1933–39. Streets and highways were the most common PWA projects."

The View

Looking south over headlands and bays from the West Shelter high up on Cape Perpetua.

CHAPTER 10

~~~~

Tolls vs Free

THE ORIGINAL agreement with the PWA for the construction of the five bridges stipulated that the federal government would grant the state $1,402,000 [30 percent], and loan the state $4,200,000 [70 percent] secured through bonds and payable through toll revenues.

The idea of tolls began back in June 1932, when the Oregon Coast Highway Association met, and Sam Dolan, an engineering instructor at OSAC, suggested charging tolls on the bridges as a means to help them pay for themselves. "This idea was not greeted warmly, debate ensued, and decided with popular support that tolls may be necessary," wrote historian Link.

Tolls, however, never became a popular idea. "It was estimated that a carload of five people would pay $4 in tolls alone to drive from Coos Bay to Newport and back," continued Link. In the middle of the Depression, that was a lot of money.

Even though construction had begun on all of the bridges, the toll controversy still festered. Eastern Oregonians still didn't want to pay for coastal bridges that they may never use. Western Oregonians objected to tolls because they thought the bridges were part of a state-wide highway improvement program benefiting everyone, just like other projects they had supported that had benefited eastern Oregon. They didn't think tolls were fair.

Newspapers throughout the state kept the topic alive. Segments of articles from Florence's *Siuslaw Oar* tell the tale of how the toll controversy played out.

October 26, 1934, "Highway Ass'n in Meet at Newport"

The annual meeting of the Coast Highway Association met at Newport last Friday and Saturday and the report is that it was one of the best meetings ever held by that body. Speakers from all over the state as well as the coast were present. First efforts to secure toll-free bridges were made at this meeting.

By now, the Oregon Coast Highway Association had become a power to reckon with. They were the first group that spoke for the whole coastal region, thus giving it an identity of its own. The legislature, the state highway commission, and even the Governor took notice, and within months, there was action.

February 22, 1935, "Bridges on Coast to be Toll Free"

The five coast highway bridges shall be toll free, the state highway commission decreed yesterday after a conference with Governor Martin. The $4,200,000 loan from the PWA will be paid off immediately by a bond issue, Chairman Leslie M. Scott said, and 1/2 percent general bonds issued in place of the 4 percent now hypothecated to PWA.

June 28, 1935, "Toll Free Bridges Finally Assured"

Final step in making the five coast bridges toll free was completed Tuesday as the state highway department passed a formal resolution to that effect, according to a U.P. report from Salem. The 1935 Legislature authorized the group to delete the tollgates from the bridge blueprints and left it to their discretion. The commission decided the $4,200,000 issue of coast highway bridge bonds will be refunded through sale of a similar issue of general obligation bonds. The new securities will be serial bonds to run for 15 years. R.H. Baldock, state highway engineer, estimated that the refunding move would result in a savings of $2,000,000 in interest payments. The savings will come through lower interest rates, and by reason of shorter maturities.

Gothic Influence

Stately entry pylons with their Gothic arches mark the southern entry to the Alsea Bay Bridge.

In the end, increased highway revenues gave state officials the confidence that they could pay back the loans, and the 1935 Legislature ended any ideas of collecting tolls on the bridges. With the controversies dealt with, the progress of the bridges now became the topic of daily conversation and of newspaper articles and editorials.

PART IV

THE RESULT: FIVE BRIDGES

~~~~~~

CHAPTER 11

Coast Bridges Project

IT WAS SHEER GENIUS to have the five bridges considered as just one project. Individually, they would not have all been funded under the PWA, and coastal communities would have been pitted against each other in trying to get their own bridge built. As one project, once the controversy of timber versus concrete and steel was settled, the coast region banded together on behalf of the Coast Bridges Project.

Providing PWA jobs

After the PWA approval in January 1934, bids opened a few months later. And by August construction was under way on all five bridges by different companies. Nobody wasted any time. Today, that kind of speed would be unheard of.

McCullough provided field engineers to oversee progress on each bridge construction site and, according to Hadlow, " . . . contractors employed eight hundred men on-site and another seven hundred in related jobs on the multi-bridge project. Despite the economic depression, costs for labor and materials in-

creased project estimates to $5.6 million."

Each site followed the design plans and specifications as developed by McCullough and the bridge section. And McCullough supervised construction until October 1935. At that time, BPR Chief MacDonald requested that McCullough be temporarily released from his duties as state bridge engineer to assist in Roosevelt's Good Neighbor policy in helping build the Inter-American Highway from Laredo, Texas, through Mexico and Central America to the Panama Canal. MacDonald chose McCullough because of his extensive knowledge and experience in designing economical bridges. MacDonald also realized that the Coast Bridges Project was well under way. As it turned out, all bridges would be completed less than a year after McCullough's departure.

Glenn S. Paxson became the acting state bridge engineer during McCullough's absence and received the mantle of construction superintendent on the Bridges Project. Albert G. Skelton (from that first OAC graduating class hired by McCullough) assisted as overall project engineer, and the resident engineers assisted at each of the five construction sites.

To fulfill PWA requirements, the Project was labor intensive whenever possible. "Workers used handsaws instead of power saws to cut lumber for falsework and wheelbarrows instead of mechanized buckets to transport wet concrete," wrote Hadlow.

The Bridges Project did, indeed, "prime the pump" in Oregon. According to Hadlow, "It provided jobs during the Great Depression — over 2.1 million hours' employment for the bridges alone. It benefited the state's industries by consuming 16 million board feet of lumber, 54,000 cubic yards of sand, 110,000 cubic yards of gravel, and 182,000 barrels of cement. It also promised to increase future tourist revenue in both the state and the region: after construction of the bridges, tourism in Oregon jumped 72 percent in one year."

Contractors completed all five bridges in 1936 within a two-year time frame, thus forging the last links in the long-awaited Oregon Coast Highway. This strengthened local economies and helped transform many fishing villages into tourist destinations.

Building solid foundations

Coastal travelers saw the graceful new bridges spanning the river bays and estuaries, and admired the central steel sections spanning the channels and the concrete arches both above and below the road deck. If they looked closely, they saw the beauty and symmetry of the architectural embellishments. What they couldn't see were the foundations hidden below the water, which represented tremendous amounts of planning and effort.

The foundations were constructed for the most part in sand with swift river currents to contend with. Each site — Newport, Waldport, Florence, Reedsport, and North Bend — presented its own particular engineering problems.

The key to building bridge foundations in water is the cofferdam. Usually constructed of strong, interconnecting sheets of steel, cofferdams provide a temporary water-free work environment for those building piers and other supports. Since the fine sands on the bottom of the estuaries constantly shifted with the tidal currents, they caused a scouring action around all obstructions — whether temporary cofferdams or permanent piers — which became a major problem. It was usually solved by filling in with rock, a.k.a. riprapping.

Another method on some of the support piers involved leaving the lower parts of the steel cofferdams in place to protect against scouring. Divers used torches that could burn under water and cut through the steel, cutting the cofferdams off as much as 10 feet beneath the water surface.

According to construction superintendent Paxson, all of the cofferdams used in the Bridges Project were made of steel sheet piling except those at the Siuslaw River Bridge. "Timber piling was used, made up of 8-by-16-inch timbers grooved on both sides."

"Some of the piers rest upon rock; others, upon sand of unknown depth," wrote Robert H. Baldock, state highway engineer, when writing about the five bridges. "Where sand is encountered, the piers must themselves be supported by piling, each driven to sustain a 20-ton load. In order to hold water out of the cofferdams that are driven in sand, an impervious floor must be provided; or, in other words, the cofferdam must be sealed. . . . It [the concrete] must be carefully conducted through a long pipe

Alsea Bay Bridge – Waldport, Ore.

Christian 474

Arches of Triumph

Deck arches in the foreground on the original Alsea Bay Bridge and tied arches above the road deck are examples of similarities in the five coastal bridges.

through the water to the floor of the cofferdam. This floor must be heavy enough to hold the cofferdam down when the water is pumped out, so that the cofferdam will not float like a tub. . . . When the pouring of the seal is started, the operation cannot be stopped until completion." The floors needed to be from three to eight feet thick, depending on the size of the cofferdams. So, a pour could last for days.

Baldock concluded, "It's an axiom among construction men that when the foundations are completed, the bridge is practically built. From then on, it's merely a matter of the joining of one piece of steel to another or the placing of one yard of concrete on top of another."

Differing designs but with similarities

At first glance, the five bridges seem like distinctly different structures, but close inspection reveals that only the middle channel spans differ. Deck arches over water or viaducts over land form the

Giant Pier

A huge newly-poured concrete pier on the Coos Bay Bridge construction site dwarfs the men standing inside. This Gothic arch, in smaller versions, is repeated on all five bridges.

approaches in each case.

According to Orrin C. Chase, one of the bridge section's design engineers, "Where it was necessary to maintain considerable vertical clearance above the water, tied arches [above road bed] were used, and where the elevation of the road was too high to admit the economical use of beam spans, fixed [deck] arches [below road bed] were adopted." Concrete was used whenever possible because of the high cost of maintaining steel.

Chase explained that the fixed-arch-on-piers design worked well for Yaquina Bay, Coos Bay, and Alsea Bay bridges. In each case, sway braces provided lateral bracing. Movement of the arches was also addressed by "welded structural steel shoes of the type ordinarily used for steel bridges," he wrote. "One shoe rests on rollers, which allows end motion."

On three of the bridges, tied arches rose above the road bed: the Alsea Bay Bridge had three in the center, the Siuslaw River Bridge one on each side of the draw span, and the Umpqua River Bridge two on each side of the steel swing span. At the ends of each of the five bridges, continuous-beam spans were used instead of arches for economical reasons.

More similarities stood out in the decorative pylons, bracketed balustrades, and other architectural embellishments as well as the Art Deco and other design motifs on flat surfaces on all of the bridges.

Although each bridge boasted a unique design, the similarities made designing the group of five easier.

Perfecting reinforced concrete

Although McCullough probably knew more about using reinforced concrete than any other bridge builder in the United States, he expanded his knowledge with each project. And that was certainly true of the Bridges Project.

Concrete for all five bridges used sand and stone aggregate obtained from river or beach deposits. Paxson explained how the mixing plants worked for the different bridges. "At the Yaquina Bay job, the mixing plant was constructed on a barge, being moved from one side of the bay to the other as the work progressed, and the concrete was transported from the mixing plant to the various parts of the project by truck. On the Alsea Bay, Siuslaw River, and Umpqua River jobs, one mixing plant [at each bridge] served the entire project, the concrete being transported across the falsework [usually by tramcars and wheelbarrow]. At the Coos Bay job, a mixing plant was erected on each side of the bay."

The Bridges Project was the first time for the bridge section to use vibrators to apply concrete instead of applying by hand. Vibrators provided a more even distribution and eliminated more air bubbles. And they saved about three-quarters of a sack of cement per cubic yard of concrete because of lower water-cement ratios possible with vibration. The results were so satisfying that the bridge section made the use of vibrators standard on all future bridgework.

Forms built for the concrete were made in sections in carpenter shops and put together on the job when practicable. In this way, carpenter work was kept to a minimum on the falsework.

To avoid excessive cracking of the concrete, the hangers and bottom chord bars were not encased in concrete until the rest of

Placing Concrete

A concrete vibrator helps in placing concrete in columns for the bascule pier on the Siuslaw River Bridge.

the structure was completely poured. Chase explained the next step: "The reinforcing bars were then welded together and the slots in the arch filled with a dry, rich concrete mix well tamped into place."

McCullough, ever conscious of the bottom line, had an on-going campaign to make reinforced concrete more economical. After trying the Freyssinet method on the Rogue River bridge and finding that it was not more economical than traditional techniques, he continued using the Considére temporary construction hinge method. He had perfected it on smaller coastal tied-arch bridges before using it on the five larger bridges. He found it reduced the amount of concrete and reinforcing steel needed in construction without requiring additional skilled labor. According to McCullough, hinges are select points in arched spans that can bend to compensate for extraordinary stresses. He wrote about them in his second book, *Elastic Arch Bridges*.

Passing test of time

Bill Calder, freelance writer and former press secretary for Senator Mark Hatfield, wrote in *Oregon Coast* magazine in 1986 that "R.H. Baldock, chief state highway engineer and then-Governor Charles Martin must also be credited [for construction of the five bridges], for both acknowledged the need to design bridges that would compliment the

Embellishment on the sway brace of the Siuslaw River Bridge.

rugged Oregon coast and its modern scenic highway." They had a sense of vision.

Baldock even referred to the new bridges as jewels. "Set like jewels in a chain of incomparable beauty, the five Oregon Coast Highway bridges will soon be open to traffic."

"True to McCullough's style, all five bridges were designed with a host of decorative features, many of which were not necessary to the function of the bridge," pointed out Calder in the same *Oregon Coast* article. But it's these unnecessary architectural embellishments that continue to amaze travelers, resulting in thousands of photographs every year.

On the day the first bridge — the Siuslaw River Bridge — opened, the Salem *Statesman* ran a prophetic editorial: "When the Depression of this decade shall have passed, the coast bridges will be there and they will have been a good investment. They will be part and parcel of a coast route, magnificent and inspiring — one to attract travelers who will recount the beauties of the coast highway in every state of the union."

Without McCullough and his particular experience with reinforced concrete and without the PWA funding available when it was most needed, these bridges would not have been built as the masterpieces they were and — except for the Alsea Bay Bridge — still are.

Yaquina Bay Bridge Embellishments

McCullough's bridges, in addition to their function, held strong to form, with decorative pylons, bracketed balustrades, and other architectural embellishments. Note the bracketed balustrade leading from the pedestrian plaza and the plaza's Art Deco and Moderne style embellishments.

CHAPTER 12

〜〜〜

Yaquina Bay Bridge

MᶜCULLOUGH THOUGHT his Yaquina Bay Bridge at Newport was one of the most beautiful of the Coast Bridges Project. "Located almost at the mouth of the Yaquina Bay, the Yaquina Bay Bridge has one of the most beautiful and spectacular settings imaginable," wrote McCullough. "Taking advantage of such a setting, a structure in keeping with it has been designed and is being constructed."

The northern bridge approach springs from the bluff about 100 feet above the bay, affording a view of Yaquina Bay to the east and the waves breaking over the bar between the jetties to the west. Because of the navigation channel's location close to the higher northern approach, the bridge could be built high enough to allow shipping traffic to pass under. And the mouth of the tidal estuary was wide enough to permit a gradual descent to the southern approach.

The design

A side view of the bridge best shows off the spectacular 600-foot steel arch that spans the navigation channel. The arch rises from piers near water level up past the road deck to 245 feet above the water. That height makes it visible for miles. This type of arch is known as a through arch, since the road deck passes through. Below the road deck, two steel deck arches — both 350 feet — flank the central span. The vertical clearance for the navigation channel measures 130 feet and the two flanking spans also allow considerable clearance. All this steel gives the bridge a light, graceful elegance.

Robert S. Cortright, author of *Bridging: Discovering the Beauty of Bridges* and a big fan of McCullough, wrote, "While most of McCullough's bridges are executed in reinforced concrete, two of the most notable spans [Yaquina Bay and the one over Coos Bay] are primarily steel. Both of these examples include concrete approach arches typical of his style, but [in each] the main span is steel."

On the southern end of the Yaquina Bay Bridge, five secondary reinforced-concrete deck arches provide support. They vary in length from 160 feet to 265 feet and are followed by 549 feet of reinforced concrete viaduct (the portion of the bridge usually

Temporary Falsework

A work bridge (top) extended out from each side, keeping an opening in the navigation channel for river traffic. Much wood (below) was used for scaffolding and forms for pouring concrete.

over land). Supporting the viaduct, short spans repeat the arch shapes and these are followed by Gothic-style supports. At the much shorter northern end, 245 feet of viaduct immediately follows the steel span with no intervening reinforced-concrete arches. The entire length of the bridge totals 3,223 feet — second longest of the five bridges.

At both ends, 51-foot pedestrian plazas provided a stopping place for travelers to see the bridge up close and to enjoy views of the bay, ocean, and portions of Newport. Elaborate curved stairways from the plazas led to landscaped waysides at each end, for which CCC workers were responsible. More than one set of pylons graced the bridge. The pairs flanking the central arch are particularly impressive as they are extensions of the massive piers with vertical scoring (fluting) enhancing their height. Other architectural details included a continuation of the Gothic-style arches in the handrails and graceful, curved brackets that support the sidewalk beneath the rail posts. Art Deco and Moderne-style detailing on the reinforced concrete surfaces completed the artistic embellishments.

The job

Bids were received for building the bridge on May 17, 1934, and the contract was awarded to the Gilpin Construction Company of Portland and General Construction Company as a joint venture. General Construction, founded in 1910 in Spokane, later acquired Gilpin and went through numerous name changes and mergers before changing back to its former name of General Construction Company. It is now one of the major construction companies in Washington state and has been involved in some of the largest bridge construction projects in the Northwest and along the Pacific coast, including the new Alsea Bay Bridge 1988–91.

Gilpin and General hit the ground running. The contract was awarded on July 25 and work began August 1. "At the beginning of the project, the contractor built work bridges to provide construction access to the portions of the bridge outside of the navigation channel and a railway along the north shore to deliver materials," wrote Ray Bottenberg in *Bridges of the Oregon Coast*. "The estimated cost of right-of-way, location surveys, field engineering, and contract items was $1,380,457.25." Actually, the project ended up costing less — $1,293,219.66.

An average of 220 men employed 30 hours a week cost approximately $5,000 each week. "Construction removed 19,830 cubic yards of earth and consumed 54,000 cubic yards of gravel, 96,191 lineal feet of piling, 28,021 cubic yards of concrete, 2,192,269 pounds of reinforcing steel, and 3,819,051 pounds of structural steel," wrote Bottenberg.

Those in charge for the contractors included Otto Hermann, superintendent, and Al McEachern, assistant superintendent; for the PWA M.E. Reed, resident engineer inspector; and for the state bridge section R.A. Furrow, resident engineer, and Ivan Merchant and R.G. Barnes assistant resident engineers.

The problems

This bridge was one of two located very close to the ocean. Because of being right at the edge, summer afternoon winds and winter storms were especially fierce. Winter storm winds regularly reached 50 miles per hour or more and several workdays

Steel Deck Arches

These steel deck arches have been completed prior to building the large steel center arch.

Almost There

The construction of the 600-foot central arch kept everyone's attention riveted for two months as the two ends gradually extended from water level to high in the air.

were lost because of "inclement weather," according to weekly reports submitted by superintendent Paxson.

"The structural steel workers," wrote Ray Bottenberg, "normally did not work on windy days; they had little of the safety equipment taken for granted today. By comparison, the concrete workers worked during the windy days when the steel workers did not, and the one known fatality during the construction of Yaquina Bay Bridge occurred when laborer Ted McDaniel fell from the falsework of the south reinforced concrete deck arch spans on a windy day, July 22, 1936."

One of Paxson's reports recounted that during a storm on January 11, 1936, the barge with the concrete plant broke loose from its moorings and ended up across the bay grounded on a beach. As it turned out, the concrete plant incurred no damage and, apparently, neither did the portions of the bridge encountered on its journey.

If you stand about the midpoint of the main span and look down 138 feet, you can't help but notice the large main piers. Because of the strong currents, it was necessary to build large temporary cofferdams to hold the water away while the piers were under construction. Both piers extend 50 feet below the water surface. The southern pier would've rested on sand. So piling had to be driven 40 feet below the channel bed to provide footings for the pier. It took approximately 700 wooden piling. (That's not a typo; 700 is correct.) With the piling in place, the cofferdam was constructed of steel sheeting, and wasn't without its problems. "The cofferdam at the pier south of the navigation channel was chronically leaky and eventually suffered a dangerous 'blow-in,' " wrote Bottenberg.

The northern pier (No. 2) rests on rock. "Swift currents posed an incredible challenge in placing Pier No. 2, which required a 100-hour continuous pour of 2,200 yards of concrete. When a concrete pour began, it continued 24 hours a day no matter how bad the weather," wrote Steve Wyatt in the *Bayfront Book*.

The work

As a major construction project, a typical day had several jobs taking place simultaneously. Here's a snapshot of what was happening during the last week of January 1936 — a typical week midway through construction. Crews worked on pouring concrete for handrails, completing the erection of falsework towers at the main northern pier, placing cable ties on the main southern pier to facilitate erection of the south side of the main span, pulling steel sheet piling from a pier, and working on constructing beam and road deck forms where arches below were far enough along.

The construction of the 600-foot central arch kept everyone's attention riveted for two months as the two ends gradually extended from water level to the height of 245 feet, heading toward each other. Finally, on March 18, 1936, the upper members of the arch rib were connected to become one continuous parabolic arch. The temporary towers with their support cables for the two extended sections were no longer needed and neither were the derricks and platforms used by the steel workers located high in the air at the ends of each extended section.

Fast-forward five months for a snapshot of a typical week in mid-August, closer to the end of construction. Crews worked on driving steel fender piling for the protection of pier 2, complet-

Sky Walker

On March 18, 1936, the upper members of the arch rib were connected, to become one continuous arch. What an exciting place to be!

Spanning Yaquina Bay

A side view of the bridge best shows off the spectacular 600-foot steel arch that spans the navigation channel. The arch rises from piers near water level up past the road deck to 245 feet above the water. That height makes it visible for miles.

ing pours on entry pylons at piers 2 and 3, completing one section of handrail and starting two more sections, stripping away wooden forms on the concrete arches followed by finishing crews smoothing and polishing the concrete, applying the final coat of three coats of paint on the two 350-foot steel arches, and hauling road surfacing material onto the bridge.

The dedication

With the road surfacing finished and the approaches on either end completed, Yaquina Bay Bridge opened to traffic on September 6, 1936, which marked the completion of the last of the five bridges of the Coast Bridges Project. The dedication ceremony, held October 3, 1936, had a distinctly military flavor with two destroyers, a squadron of seaplanes, the Seventh Infantry Band, and a company of soldiers from Fort Vancouver participating, according to the *Port Umpqua Courier.* This celebration not only commemorated the completion of the bridge, but also the completion of the last link of the Oregon Coast Highway. At long last!

The past 75 years

Because it rises so high, the Yaquina Bay Bridge is an exciting bridge to drive across. And because of its setting and impressive main span, it has become one of the most photographed bridges on the coast. Its silhouette at sunset is an iconic coastal image. Of course, Newport claims the bridge as its own and it's become the city symbol.

Although the bridge celebrates its 75th birthday in 2011, it should stand proud and provide transportation across Yaquina Bay for decades to come. The bridge underwent the impressed current zinc cathodic protection and restoration in three phases. The first in 1986 treated the northern approach, the second from August 1992 to February '94 treated the bridge arch spans, and the third from 1996 through '97 treated the southern approach spans. This high tech treatment that involves restoration of the concrete, coating with zinc, and running electricity continuously through the bridge to short circuit the corrosion of the steel rebar should ensure the bridge's integrity far into the future.

Grand Entry

The driver's view of the impressive entry pylons guarding the central arch.

Bay Blocked by Bridge Work

The work bridge extended the entire width of Alsea Bay.

CHAPTER 13

~~~

Alsea Bay Bridge

THE ALSEA BAY BRIDGE, containing no steel spans, was totally constructed of reinforced concrete. The bridge had the distinction of being the largest reinforced concrete tied-arch bridge ever designed by McCullough. According to the authors of *Historic Highway Bridges of Oregon,* "The overall appearance of the Alsea Bay Bridge is one of grace, rhythm, and harmony with the marine setting. . . . [It] is considered by some experts to rank among the finest examples of concrete bridge construction in America. The structure was determined eligible for the National Register in March 1981." But after 55 years of wear and tear and deterioration, it needed to be replaced, and it was in 1991. Here's the story behind the original Alsea Bay Bridge.

The site for the Alsea Bay Bridge sprang from a high bluff on the northern approach similar to the Yaquina Bay Bridge. Also similar were grand views: to the east the Alsea River valley and to the west the ocean. Alsea Bay was bordered on the south by the town of Waldport, which was then a port of call to numerous small fishing craft.

The design

A vertical clearance of 70 feet above low water had been provided under the three tied arches that spanned the navigation channel. The central arch had a span of 210 feet and the arches on either side each had spans of 154 feet. But this was not the original plan, according to Bottenberg in *Bridges of the Oregon Coast.* "The United States War Department," he wrote, "objected to the original proposed design, which had only one opening for marine traffic, a single reinforced concrete tied arch. So C.B. McCullough and his designers raised the critical clearance from 50 feet to 70 feet and added two more tied-arch spans."

On each end of the three tied arches, three concrete deck arches each 150 feet long were part of the design. Three arches below road level on each side of three arches above road level created a balance that was pleasing to the eye. On the northern high bank side, the arches were connected to the highway by two concrete girder spans totaling 114 feet. On the long stretch across the tidal flats to the southern approach, a concrete viaduct 1,354 feet long had numerous Gothic-style supports that had a cathedral-like quality when viewed from below. The viaduct terminated in an entrance plaza 108 feet long with stairways that gave access to the beach. The length of the bridge totaled 3,011 feet. Decorative embellishment included fluted entry pylons and

1746 2-8-35 (35)

Bundles of Brush

Thousands of bundles of brush, weighted down with bagged concrete, were placed underwater around all foundation supports to help prevent scouring.

pairs of obelisks with spires of slender tapered Port Orford cedar tips at each end of the three tied arches.

The job

"The original engineer's estimate of $685,040 was increased before award of the contract to account for 'several expensive revisions to foundations on this job,'" wrote Ray Bottenberg. "The $778,260.73 contract for construction of the bridge was awarded on April 26, 1934, to Lindstrom and Feigenson and Parker and Banfield — a joint venture." The actual cost totaled somewhat less—$769,287.48.

The joint venture got off to a fast start. By May 1 work had begun and by mid-May a steam pile driver had already begun driving piling. By mid-July a work bridge extended far into the bay. At some point the work bridge extended completely across the bay as photos in late 1934 show. This would make it impossible for vessels of much size to pass up or down Alsea Bay. Down the center of the work bridge ran a track to make delivering materials easier.

Because this was an all reinforced-concrete bridge, a massive amount of timber for concrete forms and for falsework was needed as well as a huge amount of gravel for the concrete. According to Bottenberg, "Some, if not all, of the gravel for Alsea Bay Bridge came from the gravel plant belonging to Saxton and Looney, which was located at the mouth of Ten Mile Creek."

An average number of 150 men were employed for 30 hours per week, generating a weekly payroll that ranged from $3,000 to $4,000. "Construction of the bridge removed 8,973 cubic yards of soil and consumed 19,298 cubic yards of concrete, 71,806 lineal feet of piling, 1,884,423 pounds of reinforcing steel, and 265,204 pounds of structural steel," wrote Bottenberg.

Those in charge for the contractors included D.H. Rowe, superintendent; for the PWA A.E. Eberhart (also held same position on Coos Bay Bridge), Harold Poling, and R.F. Kellogg, resident engineer inspectors; and for the state bridge section Marshall Dresser, resident engineer, and R.A. Wanless and Frank Moore, assistant resident engineers.

The problems

The Alsea Bay Bridge, like the Yaquina Bay Bridge, was built right near the mouth of the bay. Being so close to the edge exposed the workers to the strong winds of winter storms and summer afternoons as well as the coastal fog found often right along the beach. Occasionally, the weather would get so bad that work would shut down. "Sometimes it was so foggy that from the cement mixer you couldn't see out to where you were going to pour," recalled one worker as recounted by Joe Blakely in *Lifting Oregon Out of the Mud*.

Having no solid rock in Alsea Bay on which to place the support piers, all of them rested upon the sandy bottom in depths ranging from 10 to 35 feet below the water surface. Beneath each support pier, however, solid footings had been driven. Timber piling driven 40 feet below the sand comprised the footings.

All of the bridges in the Bridges Project encountered scouring around the piers, which washes away the sand and undermines the foundation. Placing riprap around the piers usually solves the problem. But the scouring was worse at the Alsea Bay Bridge with 13 or more feet of sand scoured away as the piers were being built. So instead of placing riprap around these piers to slow down the currents, bundles of brush were used. According to Bottenberg, they were sunk using bagged concrete.

"The bundles of brush," explained Baldock in *The Oregon*

1746 10-18-35 (L2)

Showing Through the Falsework

The reinforced concrete below-road deck arches and above-road tied arches can be seen through all the wooden falsework.

Pleasing to the Eye

Three arches below road level on each side of three arches above road level created a visual balance.

Motorist article "Bridge Builders' Secrets," "decreased the velocity and caused the deposition of sand carried by the water through the brush, and thus gradually the bay bottom was built back to its original position. Several thousand cords of brush are now buried beneath the sand around the Alsea Bay Bridge." Stopping the scouring action was imperative; even today scouring is the most common cause of bridge failure in the United States, according to Bottenberg.

The work

Once the foundations were in, the bridgework consisted primarily of building forms and falsework, placing the rebar, and pouring concrete plus delivering and moving all the wood, rebar, and equipment needed. Since the whole bridge was being built of concrete, the concrete plant ran 24 hours a day. Even when it was raining and stormy, concrete continued being mixed, delivered by tramcar and wheelbarrow, and poured.

The bridge began with the south approach and gradually gained in height as it reached across the bay. As it grew higher, the falsework for the first deck arch appeared; it was just a harbinger of what was to come. By fall 1935, the entire structure looked as if it was totally constructed of wood. The arched forms of the bridge gradually began to take shape, and by November you could actually see the arches through the falsework.

As with the construction on all of the five bridges, many different jobs were going on simultaneously. A snapshot of the last week in January 1936 shows that all the falsework and forms had been removed from the three below-road, south deck arches; the falsework was just starting to be removed, forms stripped, and some finishing work begun on the above road deck tied arches; and carpenter crews were building forms and others placing rebar on the below-road, north deck arches.

Just days before the dedication in May, the concrete plant — no longer necessary — had been removed. Even after the dedication, the finish work of rubbing and polishing the concrete continued. Finally, the last of the falsework and work trestles were removed and general clean-up done. When final inspection took place June 15, the Alsea Bay Bridge was ready for traffic.

The dedication

The dedication began with a bang with fireworks on May 8 and lasted for three days with a host of activities, including boat races, a marathon Alsea Bay swim, a track-and-field meet, a ladies softball game between Corvallis and Waldport, a fly-casting exhibition by the Portland Casting Club, and diving exhibitions. Even though it wasn't the first bridge completed, it was the first dedication ceremony of the five Coast Bridges Project and it was treated as a major event. On the second day, May 9, the actual dedication occurred with Governor Charles H. Martin on hand to crown the queen, introduce the officials and organizations that had contributed to the historic event, and to dedicate the bridge. Since the bridge didn't actually open until a month later, the Governor returned to do the honors a second time.

The engineers who worked on the bridge hoped that it would last 100 years but only promised 50, and the bridge fulfilled their promise plus five.

The past 75 years

Over the years, many vehicles crossed through the arches of the Alsea Bay Bridge. With the passage of time, the reinforced concrete became unstable from exposure to the elements and piling fell victim to marine worms. The bridge deteriorated so

The Second Dedication

The new Alsea Bay Bridge was dedicated in the fall of 1991. The new four-lane structure is definitely larger than its predecessor.

Out with the Old

Demolition of the old Alsea Bay Bridge took place October 1, 1991.

In with the New

The new Alsea Bay Bridge stands alone. Begun in 1988, it opened to traffic in fall 1991.

Tied-Arch Construction

Note temporary stairs and platforms for workers to get around.

badly that it was no longer economically feasible to maintain and soon would become unsafe. Replacing it became imperative.

The new bridge, begun in the summer of 1988, opened to traffic in the fall of 1991. During construction Sidewalk Superintendent Tours were held where the public was invited to walk with someone from the project to see and hear about what was happening. Besides being good public relations, it provided a memorable experience for those who participated. After completion of the new bridge, the old bridge underwent demolition October 1, 1991.

The new bridge was designed by the engineering firm of Howard, Needles, Tammen, and Bergendoff of Bellevue, Washington, and built by General Construction Company, one of the contractors on the Yaquina Bay Bridge. The new bridge made use of modern technology and materials while preserving some of the historic character of the original.

According to Cortright who was particularly fond of the original bridge, "A concerted effort was made to design a new bridge, which would approach the aesthetic appeal of the original. The result was a fine new concrete structure, which incorporates a steel through arch with a 450-foot span." It rises 90 feet above the bridge deck. Even though the arch is steel, it doesn't look it because it's not painted green. It is painted to blend in with the reinforced concrete of the remainder of the bridge.

In order to ward off the problems that sealed the fate of the original bridge, many components were made of stainless steel, and concrete and steel features were coated with sealers to prevent salt intrusion. The piling, supporting the bridge's foundations, were made of steel and concrete (not timber this time) and reached more than 100-feet — actually into the bedrock below.

Construction of the new bridge included an interpretive center at the southern end of the bridge, featuring an exhibit of the original bridge as well as an exhibit about McCullough. And north of the bridge is a wayside where some of the decorative pylons from the original bridge are displayed.

In the U.S. Department of Transportation's 1992 Biennial Awards in Highway Design, the new Alsea Bay Bridge won the Award of Merit in Category IIIA for Major Highway Structures costing over $10 million. It's hard to believe but this "new" bridge turns 20 years old in 2011.

CHAPTER 14

~~~~~

Siuslaw River Bridge

On the Siuslaw River in the 1930s, shipping traffic was much more brisk than today. That had to be taken into consideration when designing a bridge to cross the river at the town of Florence. A high bridge was simply not going to work due to the narrow and deep shipping channel with relatively low banks on each side. Therefore, it had to be a drawbridge. McCullough decided upon a double leaf, steel bascule span where both sides lifted. When they were raised, a clear horizontal distance of 140 feet would be available.

The design

The 140-foot steel draw span in the middle flanked by two 154-foot reinforced-concrete (drive through) tied arches created an outstanding example of McCullough's design work. On either side of the tied arches, the reinforced-concrete viaducts, leading to the riverbanks, were both fairly long because the navigation channel lay near the middle of the river. The

Pier House

Note the elaborately decorated obelisk tower.

northern viaduct measured 478 feet with numerous Gothic-style supports that had the cathedral-like quality associated with the old Alsea Bay Bridge when viewed from below. The southern approach viaduct measured 650 feet and had the same Gothic-style supports. The total bridge length equaled 1,568 feet.

At each corner of the draw span sat conspicuous concrete pier houses with highly decorated obelisk-style towers. A side view of the bridge showed how each pier house is an extension from the support pier below. One pier house contained the control mechanism. When the bridge was built, it was planned for an operator to be on round-the-clock duty with office space and a place to take a nap. But due to a drop-off in river traffic, bridge tenders were never assigned full-time to the Siuslaw River Bridge.

Before the bascule leaves can be raised, many

Open Sesame!

The new Siuslaw River Bridge opens, allowing a ship loaded with lumber to pass through.

safeguards come into play, including a siren, a red light, and roadway gates that stop vehicles on both sides of the lift span.

This bridge has an unusual amount of decorative embellishments on the entry pylons, within the bracketed railings, all over the obelisk towers of the pier houses and on any flat concrete surfaces in Art Deco, Egyptian, Moderne, and Gothic motifs. Interestingly, Bill Calder writing for the *Siuslaw News* noted, "No architects were retained for the building project; all the work was done by engineers working in the drafting rooms of the state highway department's bridge section." Of course, all work had to pass the critical eyes of McCullough, and nearly all of it started with his sketches and ideas.

The job

Bids were received for building the Siuslaw River Bridge on June 7, 1934, and a contract was awarded on July 25 to the Mercer–Fraser Company of Eureka, California, the same company that built the I.L. Patterson Bridge in Gold Beach a few years before. Work began August 5, and the bridge opened to traffic March 31, 1936. The contracted price was $491,646, and the actual cost was $514,977.23. When location surveys, field engineering, and right-of-way acquisitions were added, the total tallied $527,068.67.

The construction of the bridge provided 203,570 man-hours of labor directly on the project. In addition, a large amount of labor was involved in preparing the necessary materials with which to construct the bridge.

An average of 140 men employed 30 hours a week cost approximately $3,000 each week. "Construction of the bridge removed 4,960 cubic yards of soil and consumed 9,955 cubic yards of concrete, 38,902 lineal feet of piling, 1,011,689 pounds of reinforcing steel, and 584,776 pounds of structural steel," wrote Bottenberg. And 1,500,000 lineal feet of lumber and timbers provided the temporary falsework. The operating machinery to lift the bascule leaves cost approximately $40,000.

Those in charge included for the contractor H.E. Acheson, superintendent; for the PWA William Pinkney, H.W. Hopkins, and John F. Meagher (also held same position on Umpqua River Bridge), resident engineer inspectors; and for the state bridge section Arthur Jordan, resident engineer, and A.V. Benedict and C.A. DuRette (also held same position on the Umpqua River Bridge), assistant resident engineers.

The rest of the story

For the full story behind this remarkable bridge complete with numerous anecdotes from those who helped build it, lived near it, climbed over it, and much more, turn to "Book II — The Siuslaw River Bridge: The First 75 Years."

Bridging with Scows

Notice the scows being used as temporary bridges to the "island" where work is going on in the central pier that will support the swing span. Also notice clearing done prior to the cut through the ridge on Tide Ways Island.

~~~~

CHAPTER 15

Umpqua River Bridge

THE SMITH RIVER flows into the Umpqua between Gardiner and Reedsport. The channel at the juncture of the two rivers is divided by Bolon Island — called Tide Ways Island in the mid-1930s. So the ferry that traveled between Reedsport and Gardiner left Gardiner where the town fronts on the river, went past the island because the railroad bridge built in 1916 prevented any boats of any size from traveling up the Smith River, and arrived at the ferry landing in Reedsport not far from where the boardwalk by The Discovery Center is today. It was about May 1932 when the state took over ferry service. Because ferry traffic had increased so much, two ferries started providing service on May 15, 1934. During daytime, every 15 minutes a ferry would leave both Reedsport and Gardiner and in the evening they would each leave every 30 minutes. By May 11, 1936, the ferry was opened to 24-hour service due to continued increases in ferry traffic.

While the Umpqua River Bridge was part of the Coast Bridges Project, a second smaller bridge over the Smith River, although not part of the Project, was necessary as well. Construction began October 1935 and was completed a few weeks after the larger bridge.

The island connecting the two bridges needed to have .39 mile of highway cleared, graded, and paved across the middle of it. It would not be easy as it contained a high rocky ridge along its southern edge. The original highway plan included a 550-foot tunnel through the ridge where the southern portal of the tunnel would have marked the northern approach to the Umpqua River Bridge. The tunnel project was eventually scrapped in favor of a plan to cut through the island, bringing it down to the level of the planned Umpqua River Bridge. It would turn out to be one of the heaviest cuts made on any highway in Oregon up to that time.

Because the Umpqua River supported shipping traffic through a wide shallow navigation channel, a movable span was required that could accommodate taller vessels. McCullough designed a steel through truss central span that measured 430 feet — the largest swing span structure in Oregon. "The Umpqua River Bridge is an important example of McCullough's bridge engineering accomplishments," wrote the authors of *Historic Highway Bridges of Oregon*.

The design

The steel Parker truss swing span was flanked by two, 154-

The Parker Truss Swing Span

The swing span was assembled on its own island, allowing river traffic to pass on both sides.

foot, reinforced concrete through tied arch spans on each side. This gave symmetry to the five arches with the largest — the steel one — in the middle. On the northern end, a short 84-foot concrete viaduct with two deck girder spans connected with the solid rock of the island, and at the southern end, Gothic-style supports anchored the 1,072-foot-long concrete viaduct with 21 deck girder spans on its gradual descent into Reedsport. The length of the bridge totaled 2,206 feet. Though not as ornate as some of McCullough's other bridges, the bridge had decorative bracketed balustrades and approach pylons. And when viewed from below, this bridge had the same cathedral-like quality to the Gothic-style supports as did the original Alsea Bay Bridge.

The swing span could be controlled from the tender's house located high above the road deck in the cross bracing of the arch ribs or from an auxiliary switch panel placed on the sidewalk in the center of the span. The swing span's original plans underwent a change, according to Ray Bottenberg. "At the request of the U.S. Army Corps of Engineers, the design was changed from a 90-degree swing to an 80-degree swing, presumably to better match the navigation channel when the drawbridge is open."

On this bridge, a vehicle cannot drive off into the water when the swing span is open, because gates drop and block the road and, the real stopper, foot-square metal barriers swing into place blocking both ends of the road before any mechanism can start moving the span.

The design for the other bridge, the 1,600-foot-long Smith River Bridge, involved a series of creosoted pile trestle spans, carrying a reinforced concrete deck. A 40-foot section of the bridge had been specially designed so that it could be removed to permit the passage of water craft. The river was little used for navigation, but the opening was planned for the occasional dredge or pile driver.

The job

Bids were received on June 7, 1934, and a contract was awarded on July 25 to Teufel & Carlson of Seattle. Although the contract price was $551,234, the actual cost tallied out at $566,037.97. Teufel and Carlson didn't waste any time; by July 30, work had begun.

During the construction of the bridge, an average of 125 men employed for 30 hours a week generated a weekly payroll of approximately $2,500. "Construction of the bridge removed 4,068 cubic yards of soil and consumed 10,519 cubic yards of concrete, 39,739 lineal feet of piling, 1,175,191 pounds of reinforcing steel, and 1,335,921 pounds of structural steel," wrote Bottenberg.

Those in charge for the contractors included L.G. Murray, superintendent; for the PWA Homer S. Wall, Robert Neale, and John F. Meagher (also held same position on Siuslaw River Bridge), resident engineer inspectors; and for the state bridge section, Dexter R. Smith, resident engineer, L.D. Kelsen and C.A. DuRette (also held same position on Siuslaw River Bridge), assistant resident engineers. When the Coos Bay Bridge's resident engineer, Raymond Archibald, accompanied McCullough to Central America late in 1935, Dexter R. Smith transferred to Coos Bay to take his place and L.L. Jensen of Coos Bay came to Reedsport to replace him as resident engineer.

Opening the Umpqua River Bridge to traffic was dependent upon completion of the Tide Ways Island cut and of the Smith River Bridge. Both of these projects were handled by the state under separate contracts.

One of the subcontractors on the Umpqua River Bridge,

Progress on All Fronts

Swing span is completed and reinforced-concrete tied arches are under way. Notice the ridge cut on Tide Ways Island has begun.

McLeod Brothers, provided river gravel for the concrete from about 8 miles up the Umpqua. They provided gravel also to the Siuslaw River Bridge and to the Coos Bay Bridge. While the gravel was barged to the Umpqua Bridge site, it was trucked to the other two sites.

The problems

McCullough and the resident engineers wrote about the problem of building the bridge on rock that was not bedrock: "In excavating for the piers of the Umpqua bridge structure, great slabs of rock, which had spalled off from the island were found many feet beneath the surface of the river. These slabs of rock were not large enough to support the piers and yet they were so large that piling could not be driven through them. In order to break up these rock slabs, holes were drilled, powder placed through iron pipes, and the rocks were blasted out of the way."

Marine vessels had no trouble traveling up or down the river, as the swing span was constructed in the open position. It did, however create a problem for those working on the span, as it was an island in the river. A work bridge was created when needed by placing two scows such that they created a pontoon bridge, which allowed trucks to provide concrete continuously for the long pour on the seal of the massive pier in the center of the swing span. That pour required 80 hours of continuous pouring. It was one of the largest pours of the five bridges, and the pontoon bridge worked just fine.

The Umpqua River flooded on January 14, 1936, and a heavy accumulation of driftwood collected at the northern end of the partially completed bridge. According to superintendent Paxson's weekly report, "The upstream protection on the south channel pier was taken out and one dolphin [a structure made of a cluster of piling that acts as a bumper to protect piers] at the downstream end of the drawrest [another name for the large fenders on either side of the swing span pier] was also taken out by drift and high water. Most of the piling in these were salvaged, and the drift was cleared as rapidly as possible."

Tide Ways Island had a ridge 180 feet high of which 140 feet had to be removed in a swath 600 feet long and 400 feet wide at the top, with gradual slopes to reduce risk of slides. But, first, trees had to be cut and stumps and rocks blasted to create a roadway across the island to get the excavation equipment in. This was under way by March 1935, while the Umpqua River Bridge was under construction. Some of the fill was dumped in boggy areas on the northern end of the island. Most of the fill, however, would be needed for the half-mile long southern approach to the Umpqua River Bridge.

In the fall of 1935, while one of the ferries was passing under the partially completed bridge, a 2-by-4 fell and struck a Eugene man on the ferry and knocked him unconscious. Fortunately, first aid treatment revived him.

By February 1936, the Umpqua River Bridge was able to handle traffic. One of the first vehicles to cross was a huge 45-ton gasoline-powered shovel, heading to Tide Ways Island to work on the cut. Since it was too heavy for the new bridge, it had to be partially dismantled and moved over in two trips. Then Tide Ways Island contractor E.C. Hall's three brand new International tandem-drive trucks with eight-cubic-yard, side-dump boxes (to make dumping from the trestle easier) got to work. They ran three shifts a day to handle the 90,000 cubic yards needed. "Hauling approximately 100 cubic yards of fill material per hour for five months left the bridge dirty," wrote Bottenberg, "and in late July 1936, Hall's crew cleaned it, removing several tons of

Ready or Not

The road cut through the ridge on Tide Ways Island wasn't finished until August although the road had been open to Oregon Coast Highway traffic since July 2.

material with brooms, scrub brushes, and a fire hose." What a way to christen a brand new bridge!

The fill material being trucked across the bridge was needed to build up the southern approach that extended to the Scholfield Slough Bridge. During this time some settling took place at the southern end possibly exacerbated by the constant strain of heavy loads passing over. One of the Gothic-style supports moved about 6 inches off grade and had to have its columns cut free from the road deck and jacked back to grade, blocked into position, and later, after no more settling was detected, the rebar was welded and the open section closed with concrete.

The Umpqua River Bridge construction job was not without fatalities — three men died in separate accidents.

The work

By October 1934, a concrete plant, work bridge with cranes and hoisting rigs in place, and a steam driven pile driver showed plenty of activity. At this point it was mostly foundation work, building cofferdams and forms for piers, but construction of some of the land-based Gothic-style supports for the southern approach had also begun.

The tied-arch falsework was under way by January. Throughout 1935 falsework and concrete forms were built and concrete poured for the tied arches on both sides of the swing span, and construction continued on the many Gothic-style supports on the southern end. The reinforced-concrete decks came later in 1935, as did the pouring of the tied-arch deck hangers. The hangers were poured last to minimize built-in stresses. Much of this was similar to what was happening at the other Coast Bridges Project sites.

But what was happening in the middle of the river was unique to this site. The large pier for the swing span was constructed in the center of where the span would be and large pier protection fenders were also constructed extending east and west. The fenders were completed by the end of March 1935. And by May everything was ready to assemble the swing span in place above the fenders. First the falsework and then came the assembly of the steel trusses while the navigation channel remained open, usually on both sides. Construction of the 430-foot steel truss swing span took approximately five weeks.

As 1935 ended, the Umpqua River Bridge was looking more and more finished. By then deck slabs and sidewalks were being poured, and on the swing span, the steel guardrail was being riveted into place. Meanwhile, the Smith River Bridge was just revving up with piling being driven. Although the northern end of Tide Ways Island had fill dumped into its boggy areas early on in the project, the area kept settling and fill had to be dumped again and again. This was right where the new road would meet the Smith River Bridge.

By February 1936, the last concrete pour took place on the Umpqua River Bridge and removal of falsework and finishing the concrete shifted into full swing. Trucks hauled in hundreds of yards of riprap for placement around the piers. By March, the bridge was finished except for working out the kinks in the mechanism on the swing span. And, on April 7, the final inspection was made. The Umpqua River Bridge although finished, could not open to traffic of the Oregon Coast Highway because neither the southern approach nor Tide Ways Island was ready.

Opening and postponed dedication

The Smith River Bridge was completed in late May and, by

All Cleaned Up

After its scrubbing in late July 1936, the bridge looked once again like a brand new bridge. Notice the embellishments on the entry pylons.

then, the big cut was down to its last 10 feet. The loads of fill for the southern approach came to an end in July and the big cut and road through Tide Ways Island were finished in August. In the middle of all this, the Umpqua River Bridge in its not-so-clean condition opened to traffic of the Oregon Coast Highway on July 2. "Opened July 2 Without Ceremony" was the headline in the *Port Umpqua Courier*. Ferry service was discontinued the same day. The ferry used in Coos Bay moved to the Umpqua to transport gravel for the gravel plant, and its captain, John H. Graham, became the bridge tender for the new Umpqua River and Siuslaw River bridges.

The dedication had been originally planned for June 19 and then moved to July 4, but only a couple of weeks before, it was postponed. The reasons included the chamber of commerce having a very full agenda, it was getting too late to get a prominent speaker, enough housing for a large crowd would be difficult to find, and whatever they did would look like child's play compared to the gala celebration of only a few weeks earlier for the Coos Bay Bridge, reported the *Courier*. When rumor reached Reedsport that President Roosevelt would be on the Pacific Coast in September, however, the chamber sent a letter inviting the President to speak at their bridge dedication. It wasn't long before Mayor E.H. Ford received a response from Stephen Early, Assistant Secretary to the President. The White House had received the letter, the *Courier* reported. Apparently, West Coast travel plans had not been made yet, but they would keep the letter in mind when they were. So the dedication was postponed indefinitely.

Although no dedication took place, two commemorative events did actually happen. Teufel & Carlson bridge contractors held a picnic on Labor Day 1935 for everyone working on the Umpqua River Bridge, including workers' families, and the *Courier* had a 32-page Special Bridge & Development Issue on September 25, 1936.

The past 75 years

Although the Umpqua River Bridge is the Rodney Dangerfield of the five coast bridges and hasn't received the respect and attention that the other bridges have, it continues to do the job it was built to do — carry vehicular traffic continuously and open occasionally to let larger marine traffic through. Its decorative concrete balustrades are still impressive and its Gothic-style supports when viewed from below continue to evoke a cathedral-like ambiance. In 2005, the Umpqua River Bridge was placed on the National Register of Historic Places, and in 2011, it turns 75. Its future, like the other reinforced-concrete coast bridges, is dependent on receiving the cathodic protection and restoration treatment. According to ODOT officials, the Umpqua River Bridge is on the schedule, but it will be several years in the future because it's turn comes last after the Siuslaw River Bridge.

Its companion bridge, the Smith River Bridge, carried traffic until 1999 when it was replaced with a reinforced-concrete structure.

McCullough's Favorite Bridge

The completed Coos Bay Bridge is slightly more than a mile long.

CHAPTER 16

~~~

McCullough Memorial Bridge

THE MCCULLOUGH MEMORIAL BRIDGE was originally named the Coos Bay Bridge because it crossed Coos Bay between Russell Point on the north and Simpson Park to the south within the city of North Bend. Not only was it the longest of the five bridges of the Coast Bridges Project, but at 5,305 feet, it was the longest structure on Oregon's entire highway system at the time it was built. The bridge's steel cantilevered truss midsection is flanked on both sides by numerous reinforced-concrete deck arches and exhibits an array of architectural and decorative features. David Plowden, an acclaimed photographer and critic of bridge design, labeled this bridge, "An outstanding example of the large steel cantilever." In his book, *Bridges: The Spans of North America*, he states, "Few later bridges of its type have been as outstanding."

The design

Because of the large amount of shipping in the Port of Coos Bay, a bridge high enough to clear large vessels was needed. With Coos Bay's great width and 40-foot-high approaches, it would be possible to build a high bridge. McCullough envisioned a bridge ascending high enough to provide 150 feet of vertical clearance.

So he designed a steel cantilever truss, 793 feet long, spanning the main channel, supported by steel towers on either end of the channel. Balancing the load on each side of the cantilever would be the anchor spans also of steel, measuring 457½ feet long, making a total length of 1,708 feet of steel truss. This central steel section, longer than the entire Siuslaw River Bridge, was considered an engineering marvel at the time.

Thirteen reinforced-concrete deck arches (below the road deck), similar to those on the Yaquina Bay and original Alsea Bay bridges, flanked both sides of the steel midsection. Like the Siuslaw River Bridge, the navigation channel's location was near the center of the bridge, affording long approaches on both sides. The northern approach consisted of seven reinforced-concrete deck arches, varying in length from 151 to 265 feet, followed by 492 lineal feet of reinforced-concrete deck girder viaduct and ending at a plaza 57 feet long. The southern approach consisted of the remaining six reinforced-concrete deck arches, varying in length from 170 to 265 feet, followed by 233 lineal feet of reinforced-concrete deck girder viaduct and ending at a plaza 51 feet long. The total length of the bridge measured slightly more than a mile.

Lots of Reinforcing

Reinforced concrete contains reinforcing steel, commonly referred to as rebar, and the south cantilever pier contained lots.

According to the authors of *Historic Highway Bridges of Oregon*, "To ease design conflict between the steel truss and the arch spans, the cantilever was constructed with curved upper and lower chords [the main top and bottom structural members of a truss bridge]."

And true to form, the bridge boasted architectural embellishments, including curved sway bracing of the steel truss (what the driver sees above him), which gave the impression of traveling through a series of Gothic-style arches. The concrete railings repeated the Gothic arch theme. And the tall piers supporting the end points of the steel truss also had Gothic-style arches. The plazas provided parking for cars and contained Art Deco and Moderne embellished abutments and graceful staircases, descending to park areas below. McCullough always took into consideration what could be seen from below. "McCullough paid close attention to all the piers' shape and form," wrote Hadlow, "because he knew that park visitors would see them up close." Simpson Park was below the bridge to the south and later McCullough Wayside was added to the north.

The job

This was the most complicated bridge of the Coast Bridges Project because of its size, complexity, and dovetailing of more than one contracted job. Bids were received April 26, 1934, and contracts awarded July 25. The contract for the steel cantilever span, including concrete deck, was awarded to Virginia Bridge & Iron Company of Roanoke, Virginia, for $593,880. The contract for the remainder of the structure went to Northwest Roads Company of Portland for $1,529,438. The total amount of contracts equaled $2,123,318, and the actual cost tallied out to an incredibly close $2,126,132.29.

Work began within a few days when a Northwest Roads pile driver mounted on a barge powered by a steam donkey engine started driving piling for a work bridge. Traveling derricks would move along the work bridge to deliver and hoist materials as needed.

An average of 250 men employed 30 hours a week cost approximately $7,000 each week. "Construction of the bridge removed 24,331 cubic yards of soil and consumed 48,425 cubic yards of concrete, 209,895 lineal feet of piling, 5 million board feet of lumber for falsework, 4,337,571 pounds of reinforcing steel, and 7,505,803 pounds of structural steel," wrote Bottenberg.

Subcontractor American Bridge Company fabricated the components for the steel cantilever truss. Those in charge among the three companies doing the actual construction included Northwest Roads Company's E.C. Panton, superintendent; Virginia Bridge & Iron Company's H.E. Robertson, representative; and F.L. Holser Company's (under subcontract for erection of the steel) William Kelly, superintendent. Those in charge for the PWA included S.M.P. Dolan and A.E. Eberhart (also held same position on the Alsea Bay Bridge), resident engineer inspectors; and for the state bridge section Raymond Archibald, resident engineer, and L.C. Smitton, L.L. Jensen, and O.R. Kennen, assistant resident engineers.

The problems

The bridge worksite measured over a mile long and one temporary construction bridge stretching from one end to the other would not be possible because of the shipping traffic. Boats helped solve the problem of getting from one worksite to another. To keep the shipping traffic moving between the work bridges without bumping into them, pier protection dolphins made up

#133 4-30-35

Pier Protection

The south cantilever pier (containing all that rebar) rises at the edge of the navigation channel. Note the pier protection dolphins made up of bundles of 70-foot-long piling.

A Mile of Progress

Deck arches show various stages of construction, and the southern segment of cantilever shows progress.

of several bundles of four or five 70-foot-long piling were driven in spaced several feet apart around the end of each work bridge.

A cantilevered bridge is built by projecting out from a supporting pier on one side while maintaining a counterbalance on the opposite side to keep the first side from tipping over into the bay. That meant that whatever was done on the north side had to be done on the south or counterbalancing side or have supports in place, either temporary or permanent. And this whole process was repeated 793 feet away on the other side of the navigation channel. Building two cantilevered trusses and then having them connect precisely in every way in the middle to complete the 1,708-foot steel truss took endless, careful planning. It helped that each counterbalance side had a work bridge underneath where temporary supports could be used.

And, of course, the weather played havoc with schedules. Wet steel meant slippery steel, so dozens of workdays were lost as work was postponed due to rain. Wet steel can't be painted either; what would have taken a few weeks in dry weather took closer to 10 months.

Wind was factored into the design of all the bridges. According to Cheryl Landes in "McCullough Bridge: Engineering as Art" in *Oregon Coast* magazine, "To keep the bridge in place in case of high winds, it was fitted with 'wind anchor shoes.' Roller bearings allow the steel span to move a few inches back and forth with temperature changes. These wind shoes sit on top of the concrete pillars [piers] and penetrate the steel above, allowing the bridge to slide back and forth but not side to side."

Landes also recounts a humorous power-of-the-wind story: "Once when a huge crane on the north trestle [work bridge] was being moved, a gust of wind snatched it away from the work crew and blew it at about twenty miles per hour toward a wait-ing truck. The huge crane stopped a few feet before it reached the truck, well ahead of its pursuers, who could only watch with open mouths and scratch their heads in wonder."

The work

After the work bridges were completed, it was essential to get the four main piers in place so that the cantilevered steel trusses could be built. The two piers flanking the navigation channel were not the tallest piers, but would be located where the steel towers anchored the cantilevers. The bases of each of these main piers measured 43 feet by 90½ feet, and 608 piling supported each pier. The two other large piers were taller and were designed with Gothic-style arches. They marked the north and south end points of the steel trusses at road deck height. These end points marked the portals where vehicles entered and left the steel truss section.

In mid-May 1935, the first piece of structural steel was carefully set atop the main pier south of the navigation channel, beginning the south cantilever. As the trusses underwent assembly above and below road deck level, road deck construction took place simultaneously. From a distance it may have looked like assembling pieces of an erector set, but these steel truss members were extremely heavy, so derricks with booms, lots of rigging, and stabilizing guy wires were all part of the scene. And many block-and-tackle setups lifted and lowered buckets filled with supplies and tools. The south cantilever reached its south pier end point 465 feet to the south by August. Because of that length, a temporary support was installed midway. Facing north, the south cantilever reached 220 feet, which is where work halted until the second cantilever could get to the same point and they would meet.

The steel tower for the north cantilever reached its full height

Steel Workers in the Fog

Weather sometimes made it more difficult for steel workers working on the cantilever truss sections on the McCullough Memorial Bridge.

Almost There

The two cantilever sections are getting closer. The southern deck arches are nearing completion, but the northern ones have a long ways to go.

by mid-September, at which time, work could begin on extending it north and south. By mid-November, the north cantilever reached its north pier end point. And by December 6, 1935, the two cantilevered sections met and became one single truss section.

Meanwhile the 13 reinforced-concrete arches took shape as crews built cofferdams, piers, falsework, and placed reinforcing steel and poured concrete. Because there were so many arches, they were all in various stages of completion throughout 1935. Much of 1936 was taken up with finish work: dismantling falsework and forms, polishing concrete, finishing the smaller supports at each end of the bridge, building the approaches, constructing the road girder viaduct sections, building the plazas, finishing the concrete rails, pouring sidewalks, and dismantling all temporary apparatus. The bridge opened to traffic May 5, and all work on the bridge was completed by July 4. The work bridges weren't totally dismantled until mid-September.

The dedication

The bridge held its dedication ceremony during a three-day celebration June 5 through 7, 1936, which included coronation of a queen, parades, foot races, banquets, a Seattle orchestra, a log-bucking contest, fireworks, a trap shoot, and an outdoor religious service. The *Port Umpqua Courier* reported that the parade featured various stages of the development of transportation, including a covered wagon with two oxen, a six-horse stagecoach, and several early models of cars.

As quoted in Joe R. Blakely's *Lifting Oregon Out of the Mud*, at the dedication ceremony, Governor Martin affirmed with great pride, "More than a mile in length with its great steel cantilever truss elevated 150 feet above the main channel and with a central span of 793 feet, the construction of this bridge is an engineering triumph, a symbol of human genius, courage and effort."

The past 75 years

The bridge has become one of the most recognizable icons of the Oregon coast and is the symbol for North Bend. In 1947, the bridge was dedicated posthumously to Conde B. McCullough and renamed the Conde B. McCullough Memorial Bridge. The wayside north of the bridge is now called the Conde B. McCullough State Recreation Site. In 2005, the bridge received recognition through placement on the National Register of Historic Places.

On December 4, 1986, bridge travelers were inconvenienced for six weeks when a ramp connected to a ship hit one of the bridge supports, and some of the bridge's understructure had to be repaired. They found that instead of taking a few minutes to cross the bay on the bridge, they needed about 45 minutes to drive around the bay.

By 2007, the average daily traffic had grown to 15,150 vehicles.

Currently the bridge is undergoing Phase 1 of eight to nine years of improvements. Phase 1 includes the impressed current zinc cathodic protection and restoration process on the southern section of the bridge as well as repaving the road deck, painting the steel portion, and replacing the concrete handrails on the southern section. This phase was scheduled to last approximately four years and will be completed in 2011.

Phase 2 covering the northern section will begin soon after and is estimated to take five years, if funding falls into place. With the restoration and other improvements along with the application of the zinc coating with the electrical current to protect against the corrosive effects of the salt air, the McCullough Memorial Bridge should be around for decades to come.

Conde B. McCullough Memorial Bridge

Photos clockwise from top:

The plaque commemorating Mc-Cullough when the bridge was re-named; the view through the Gothic arches from below the bridge on the southern end; and one of three highly embellished stairways leading from the plazas at both ends of the bridge.

McCullough After the Bridges

BEFORE MCCULLOUGH left for Central America, a banquet was held in his honor in Portland, where the table decoration was especially appropriate, explained Onno Husing. It featured an ice sculpture of Gold Beach's I.L. Patterson Bridge.

McCullough's trip to Central America was precipitated by the United States and other governments in the Pan-American Union pressing for construction of the Inter-American Highway. The road would connect the Central American countries of Guatemala, El Salvador, Honduras, Nicaragua, Costa Rica, and Panama. Eventually, it would become part of the Pan-American Highway, extending from Alaska, to the tip of South America.

"McCullough and Raymond Archibald, one of McCullough's design engineers who had also worked in Central America for the U.S. Bureau of Public Roads (BPR), left Salem in December 1935 for San Jose, Costa Rica," wrote Hadlow, "where they worked on the design of many structures for the proposed route,

Conde B. McCullough

including three short-span suspension bridges."

The suspension bridges spanned the "Rio Tamasulapa in Guatemala, Rio Choluteca in Honduras, and Rio Chiriqui in Panama" according to Hadlow. "The first two are still standing, and the last one was destroyed in the 1980s."

After his return in the spring of 1937, McCullough did not rejoin the bridge section. Instead, the state highway commission promoted him to full-time assistant state highway engineer, a post he had filled part time since 1932. His job was basically administrative; he oversaw highway and bridge construction, maintenance, budgets, and project planning.

McCullough resented being "kicked upstairs" because he missed being involved in the designing and building of bridges. He did find, however, that his new job allowed him time to resume researching and writing technical reports and books, which he enjoyed. According to the authors of *Historic Highway Bridges of Oregon*, "Three [of McCullough's] technical bulletins received national recognition: *The Economics of Highway Planning, The Determination of Highway Systems Solvencies,* and *An Analysis of the Highway Tax Structure in Oregon.*"

And during the mid-1940s, McCullough thoroughly enjoyed joint authorship with his son, John, of a two-volume text titled *The Engineer at Law: A Resume of Modern Engineering Jurisprudence.* During this time, he also enjoyed leading Salem's new Long Range Planning Commission.

In late spring1946, MacDonald invited McCullough to return to Central America to help the BPR again with the Inter-American Highway, since more bridges were needed in El Salvador and Honduras. Because it offered a chance to resume building bridges, McCullough leaped at the chance.

Here, from Hadlow's book, are McCullough's own thoughts regarding the bridges he built: "Someone once asked McCullough if he was proud to 'be able to drive up and down this state and see the great highways and beautiful bridges that he helped to build.' He replied. 'You know, my good sir, if we engineers had souls, which I doubt, we might have to take to the backroads to keep from blushing every time we see some of the things we have done. But on the other hand, I'm kinda human like the rest of humanity, and I'll admit that there's at least one or two bridges I've had a hand in, and when I look at them, I kinda figure I'll have some alibi when I see Saint Peter. Not all of 'em, you understand but some of 'em did come out so good they make life worth living.'"

Just a couple of days before his planned return trip to Central America, McCullough had a massive stroke and died on May 6, 1946, less than a month before his 59th birthday.

Fourteen months later on August 7, 1947, the bridge over Coos Bay was renamed the Conde B. McCullough Memorial Bridge with a plaque inscribed with the following words: "Dedicated to the memory of Conde Balcom McCullough whose genius and inspiration are manifest in the design of this bridge and many other Oregon bridges during his period of service as bridge engineer and assistant state highway engineer 1919 to 1946."

His legacy continues. "In 1999," wrote Hadlow, "in honor of its one hundred twenty-fifth anniversary, the periodical *ENR*, once known as *Engineering News-Record,* published a list of the top people who had made outstanding contributions to the construction industry since 1874. . . . Ten bridge designers made the list, and among them was C.B. McCullough."

~~~~~~~

"...if we engineers had souls, which I doubt, we might have to take to the backroads to keep from blushing every time we see some of the things we have done. But on the other hand, I'm kinda human like the rest of humanity, and I'll admit that there's at least one or two bridges I've had a hand in, and when I look at them, I kinda figure I'll have some alibi when I see Saint Peter. Not all of 'em, you understand but some of 'em did come out so good they make life worth living."

Conde B. McCullough

Book II

~~~~~

Siuslaw River Bridge
The First 75 Years

Siuslaw River Bridge in snow

McCULLOUGH WAS INVOLVED in designing hundreds of bridges in both Iowa and Oregon, and 30 bridges in Oregon bear his name as bridge designer. But no bridge better exemplifies the characteristics that make his bridges special than the bridge in Florence over the Siuslaw River. Here is the story behind this jewel of a bridge.

The last ferry to serve Florence was Tourist I. *It was 65 feet long and usually held about 10 cars.*

PART I
CONSTRUCTION

~~~~

CHAPTER 1
Preparation & Fast Start

LONG BEFORE the actual building of a bridge, McCullough would spend time at a site, looking at it from several angles to picture the finished project. He would consider all the surveys and measurements. Then he would look at it some more before making decisions.

When it came to the Siuslaw River Bridge, he considered the topography of the surrounding country and saw that it was not practicable to place a structure high enough to clear watercraft on the river. Therefore, a drawbridge had to be built. Once he decided on the double bascule design, this meant concrete pier houses could be placed at each corner of the span to house the controlling mechanisms. And with tied arches above the road deck on each side of the bascule, he could provide additional channels through which small craft could travel. He chose the Gothic arches with their cathedral-like qualities when viewed from below to support the viaducts that connected with the north and south approaches. And he didn't stint on the aesthetic embellishments. He then gave his sketches to his staff to work out the details — of course, he had to approve everything each step of the way.

While McCullough and the bridge section were madly scrambling to design five bridges in the summer of 1933, the people of Florence were reading in *The Siuslaw Oar* that the state had been authorized to build the five bridges, which included their bridge over the Siuslaw River. Immediately, "there were questions as to how local streets should be laid out to accommodate approaches to the new structure, since the highway must feed directly onto the span," wrote author Ellen Traylor in *A Bridge Back*, a history of Florence.

Traylor goes on to show that not everything printed that summer about the coming bridge would turn out to be true. "The paper announced that it would be a high structure of three spans." Anyone who has seen the bridge knows otherwise.

And not all townspeople were happy with the coming bridge. "There were the expected naysayers," wrote Traylor, "who preferred that life go on as it always had, untouched by any changes. And homeowners near the river worried that their houses might have to be moved."

Tale of Two Houses

Notice the two houses in front of the water tower. The one on the right is the A. Pihlgron house that survived a five-block move to Laurel Street before bridge construction. The other house, the Kyle house, was later moved also and is now the Edwin K. B & B on Bay Street. The Dairy Queen is now at that location.

Most residents, however, were thrilled with the coming bridge and could hardly wait to bid farewell to the ferry. In 1933, a Florence–Eugene bus line had been established, anticipating the growth of travel to the coast with the completion of the highway. And by 1934, investors began pouring money into the local economy on news of the new bridge. Hopes for the future of Florence had never been higher.

Building approaches

Eugene's *Register–Guard* reported in November 1933 that Harry Benson would be the man in charge of securing right-of-way for the State Highway Commission to build the approaches on both sides of Florence's proposed new bridge site.

"Some of the property being sought for the right of way is owned by Lane County," said Benson, "having been taken over for delinquent taxes. There is no difficulty in securing that property, but there has been considerable delay in obtaining deeds to some of the lots owned by individuals."

Through spring and early summer, George Lammers and Sons moved houses to clear the right-of-way for the bridge approaches. All together, they moved 11 houses. "The most particular job," reported *The Siuslaw Oar*, "was that of moving the A. Pihlgron house about five blocks, making five turns. The house is plastered and has a fireplace. When it was placed on its new foundation, the plastering was not damaged and the fireplace was as good as new." That house is now at 351 Laurel Street and houses Terry James' hair salon.

In early June 1934, the highway commission purchased two hilly lots from Grant L. Colter (ferryman for the *Tourist I*) that would provide about 8,000 cubic yards of fill to be used at the Glenada end of the bridge, reported the *Oar*. After removal, the two lots would be on a level with the highway.

The lots formed a sand hill [a dune], explained the late Carl Knowles, an old-timer who worked on building the approaches.

"I worked on the building of the approaches on each side of the Siuslaw Bridge," Knowles said. "We started by clearing huckleberry, salal, and rhododendrons and piling them all up and burning the piles. Then we built the grades — the Florence grade first."

Knowles said it was much easier to build the grade on the Florence side even though it was quite long. The grade began about where Quince Street comes into Highway 101 today. On the Glenada side, it wasn't nearly as long, but it involved a big fill.

While working on the approaches, trucks were hauling a lot of sand. Some places along the grade needed to be filled and others needed to be cut. Sometimes when hauling across dry, loose sand, the trucks got stuck; they were not four-wheel drive vehicles. They were brand new Ford one-ton trucks that held about two-and-a-half cubic yards of sand with an 8-inch board on each side.

During part of the time that Knowles was moving sand around on the Florence side, he worked with a shovel operator who scooped sand from a hill and loaded it into their trucks where it was taken only about 100 feet before being dumped. Back and forth they went. One day, the shovel operator dug into the same hill one more time, and two gallon jugs came sliding down with the sand. "The shovel operator stopped his machine, climbed down, and retrieved one of the jugs," Knowles said. "After pulling the cork and determining that it was moonshine, he told us that he would 'take care of it,' and that was the last the rest of us saw of either one of those jugs."

Fast Start

Falsework from the Glenada side stretched to the middle of the river only three weeks after the contract was awarded. Notice piling corralled and waiting their turn.

The workers took only an occasional day off, but Knowles recalls the day a few of them went crabbing.

"We rented a rowboat in Florence and went out with the tide," he said. "We stopped in a little bay that was only about five or six feet deep at low tide. In a short time, we dipped up 75 or 80 crab off the bottom with ordinary garden rakes. Then we loaded them in the boat, and when the tide came in, so did we — to Florence with our load of crab. We spent the rest of the day cooking and eating crab, and some of them got canned." Of course, you can't do that today, and that little bay is now the north jetty parking lot.

After the sand grades were built, it was time for the base rock. "The only base rock used was small round boulders," said Knowles, "about the size of cantaloupes that came from Cape Creek." Knowles drove one of the trucks that helped transport the rock to Florence. Hauling loads of this base rock by truck to the Glenada side meant using the ferry, sharing it with locals and tourists. When the ferry was full, Knowles and the other drivers had to wait until the next trip across — just like everyone else.

After the base rock came a layer of crushed rock, which Knowles said he thinks must have been brought in by barge. Then came a layer of clay for the shoulders of the new approaches, which was actually a mixture of gravel and clay — locally known as Roosevelt gravel. That came in by truck, and Knowles was involved in hauling that too.

"My job was done when it was ready for the surfacing," Knowles said.

According to the *Oar* on July 27, 1934, "Both approaches will be graveled and oiled by the contractors before leaving the job."

On August 8, the paper reported that 10 trucks began hauling gravel from Cape Creek. "The round trip to the pit was about 27 miles and each of the trucks made the round trip in an hour, hauling two and one-half [cubic] yards at a load. At this rate, both the Florence and Glenada approaches should be completed in about two weeks, except for the oiling."

Starting construction

News from the State Highway Commission, reported in the *Oar* on July 13, 1934, announced that all negotiations for the nearly $6 million loan from the government for the building of the coast bridges would be completed by July 14. That meant that construction could actually begin.

James D. Fraser, president of Mercer–Fraser, the company contracted to build the new bridge, visited Florence July 11 accompanied by H.E. Acheson, his new bridge superintendent. "While here," reported the *Oar*, "they awarded Yellow Fir Company of Cushman the contract to furnish about one-and-a-half million lineal feet of lumber and timbers, which will be used for forms and construction of the falsework."

On August 3, the *Oar* reported that the piling contract for more than 1,700 piling of mostly Douglas fir had been let to G.M. Parker of Eugene, and they would be required to have some piling on the job ready to be used by early the next week. The same issue also reported that Acheson would be on the job permanently starting the following week.

By then, Mercer–Fraser had erected an office near the southern approach in Glenada where superintendent Acheson and timekeeper C.C. Langin were indeed on the job.

"When they first started to build the bridge," old-timer Fred Jensen explained, "Trygve Nordahl went down to the [Coos] Bay Area and bought the tug *May* and brought it up to move barges

9/14/34

Glenada Building Boom

A ramp leads to where the concrete plant will be located on the Glenada side. Lots of new buildings related to the bridge construction gave Glenada a look of a boom town.

around — especially the ones that held pile drivers."

On August 9 — only two weeks after the contract was awarded — work began. The McLeod Brothers, who had been subcontracted for the work, drove the first piling for the construction of the falsework that functioned as a temporary work bridge. According to the *Oar*, "Two shifts will be employed, six men to the shift. Other men now on the payroll number 12, making a total of 24. Within a week, more men will be needed."

A couple of old-timers numbered among those employed. "Sam Seymour drove the first piling for dock improvement in Glenada in 1891, and he is one of the head pile drivers today on the bridge project," reported the *Oar*. Bill Thomas was another one, with experience also dating back decades.

A large scow load of machinery arrived August 27 from Marshfield. It held concrete mixers, hoists, cables, and power machines of various kinds. This was unloaded on the new work bridge, of which a good section had already been built.

Before long, elevated tanks, blacksmith shops, storage houses for cement, office buildings, and so forth gave Glenada the appearance of a boom town. And more men were being employed. Everyone who applied didn't get hired, but Mercer–Fraser used every man for whom it could find a place.

Married men, however, were treated differently than single men. "On this bridge project," says Jensen, "single men could work for only six months. My uncle, Mel Jensen, was single and didn't want to quit after his six months were up. So he married his sweetheart, Margaret, a year before they planned to, so that he could keep his bridge job for up to two years. And I'm sure there were many other marriages that might not have happened otherwise." Talk about marriages of convenience!

The concrete plant was built on the Glenada side. Only three weeks after the first piling went in, piling for the work bridge had been driven out to the middle of the river where the first pier on the south side would be built that would support the bascule lift span. And tramcars were already being lined up to deliver concrete. It looked like everything was falling into place to build the bridge foundation.

"On this bridge project, single men could work for only six months. My uncle, Mel Jensen, was single and didn't want to quit after his six months were up. So he married his sweetheart, Margaret, a year before they planned to, so that he could keep his bridge job for up to two years. And I'm sure there were many other marriages that might not have happened otherwise."

Fred Jensen

117

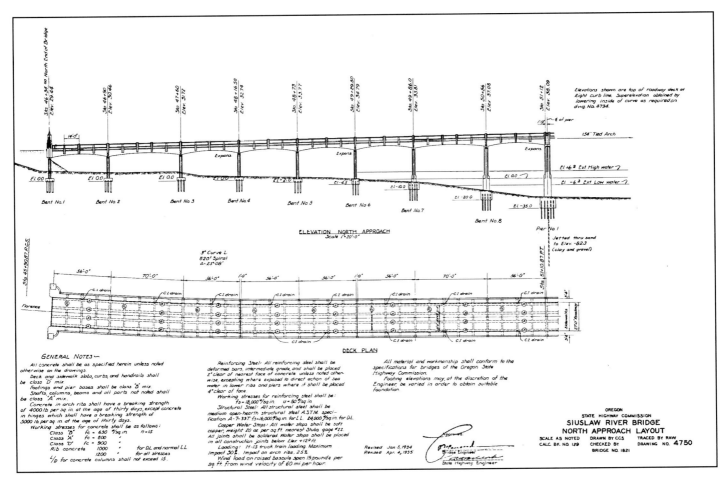

North Viaduct

Here are the eight bents and one pier of the north viaduct. Notice how each support has its own support — piling that have been pounded to a depth of 30 or 40 feet into the tidal flats or river bottom beneath it.

118

CHAPTER 2

~~~~

The Substructure

BELOW A BRIDGE'S ROAD DECK lies the most important part of the bridge — its support system, otherwise known as the substructure. It's made up of the underwater foundations and the visible piers and bents that support the bridge. Piers, a commonly used term, describes the supports located in water and bents, a not so commonly used term, describes the supports usually located on land.

The Siuslaw River Bridge has two massive piers, supporting each end of the double leaf bascule span. These had to be big — big enough to provide space for the machinery and counterweights involved in lifting both sides of the bascule lift span. On either side of these piers, smaller ones — with Gothic-style arches — help support the far ends of the tied arch spans that flank the bascule span.

But most of the bridge is supported by bents — those even smaller supports that march all the way to both ends of the bridge. They support the northern and southern viaducts — those sections of the bridge that lead from each end over land and tidal flats to the main spans over the navigation channel. Because many of these smallest supports, totaling 20, are situated on tidelands, they are sometimes standing in water. Twelve bents support the south-

ern viaduct leading to Glenada and eight support the northern viaduct to Florence. From below on Florence's Bay Street, it's easy to walk right up to four of them and look through their Gothic-style openings to obtain the cathedral-like effect.

Complex, confusing cofferdams

Nearly all the piers and bents began with cofferdams. Each pier had a large one, and some of the bents on tidal flats had two, one under each leg. Whether it was one or two, each cofferdam was filled with as many piling as could fit and these were driven by a pile driver as far down as each piling could go, usually 30 to 40 feet in this river location. These piling constituted the footing for each cofferdam, except for two that rested on rock. While most cofferdams have sides made of sheet steel, on this bridge grooved wooden planks several inches thick were used.

By mid-September 1934, piling for the work bridge had been driven out to where the large bascule pier on the southern side would be constructed, starting with its large cofferdam. In building bridges that cross water, cofferdams were (and are still) needed because they provide a water-free workspace, even while surrounded by water. Cofferdams are usually temporary but not always.

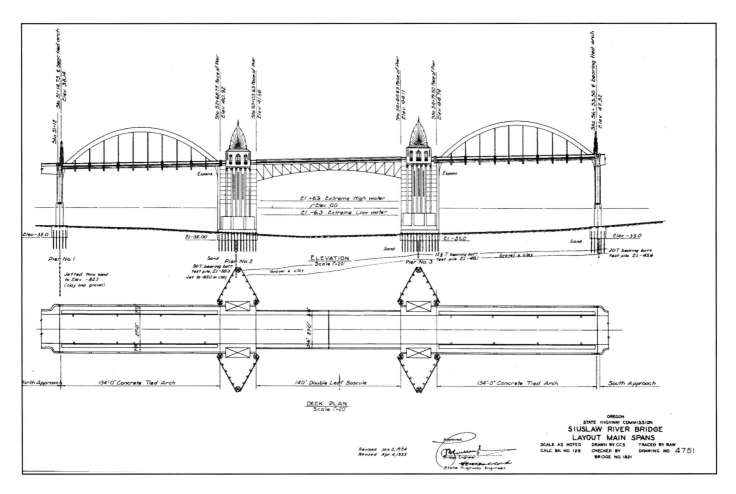

Central Spans

The two piers at the ends of the tied arches are larger than the bents, but appear small compared to the bascule piers. Hundreds of piling support each bascule pier and each bascule pier is topped with two pier houses — one on each side of the road deck.

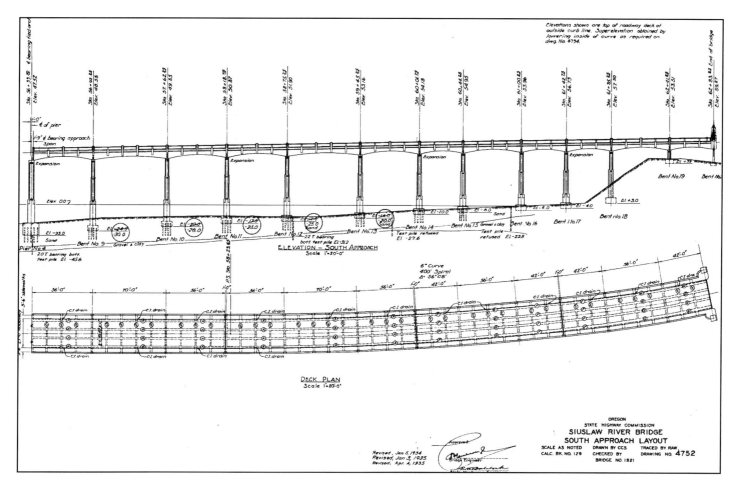

South Viaduct

Here are the 12 bents and one pier of the south viaduct. Notice how all but five have piling supporting them. Bent numbers 16 and 17 are on rock and need no piling. Bent numbers 18 through 20 are on solid ground and need a simpler, concrete foundation.

Starting on Glenada side

By September 21, piling for the work bridge seemed to stretch across the river, but it actually stopped in the middle. Later when there was a work bridge on the Florence side too, a space would be maintained for the passage of the ferry and any other river traffic. The ferry threaded its way through about every 15 minutes throughout construction. The ferry closed every night to the public just like it always had, but it stayed open for bridgework when needed.

By late September, excavating was going on at the bascule pier and another crew was beginning excavation for the smaller tied-arch pier. Although the Glenada side was where the main action was taking place, pile drivers were already starting to set piling for the work bridge on the Florence side.

Only the one concrete mixing plant on the Glenada side was constructed for the bridge project. The paper described it as "huge." The bunkers extended quite high, but concrete and gravel trucks could still negotiate the wooden ramp and dump their loads directly into the top of the bunkers. After the concrete was mixed, it then flowed by gravity to tramcars, which ran on rails — moved along by a man alongside — to the respective piers, and then to the wheelbarrow handlers.

By the end of September there were 56 men on the payroll, not counting the men from Yellow Fir Company delivering lumber and timbers on schedule. "Seems to be no hold-ups anywhere on the line," reported the *Oar*.

In most years, the weather takes a change for the worse about mid-October and 1934 was no exception. On October 26, the paper noted that, "Weather conditions have interfered somewhat with bridge work this week." Well, that was to happen from time to time for the next six months.

By the end of October — despite the weather — the bridge-building job was on schedule, according to William Pinkney, inspector for the PWA. The timber walls of the cofferdam for the bascule pier were completed, and all the piling had been driven down through the cofferdam for the tied arch pier to provide its footing. And the *Oar* reported that a submerged cable to carry power for use by the bridge contractors was installed October 25.

As an added protection to the main piers of the bridge, the thick wooden walls of the cofferdams were going to be left in place after the piers were built. Later, they would be cut off below low-water marks.

To ensure their stability for years to come, the cofferdam walls had to be secured to the concrete piers themselves. So huge spikes were driven into the heavy timbers at the base and at intervals to the water's surface, leaving several inches of spike showing to be gripped by the concrete. Diver A.G. Zimmerman spent several days driving in spikes.

By the first week in December, the cofferdams for the two piers were ready for the seals to be poured. "No water will be pumped from the cofferdams to do this work," stated the *Oar* on December 7. Then went on to explain, "The concrete hardens under water and forms a seal. In about 30 days, the water will be pumped. Piling, which have been driven below the bottom of the cofferdam excavations, will be cut off a foot or two above the seal and forms will be erected for the construction of each pier."

"The first pouring of concrete was made yesterday [December 13] and is continued today," reported the *Oar*. "The pouring is in the tied arch cofferdam and is for the seal only with a thickness of about three feet."

The new year, 1935, began with an even larger pouring. It was for the six-foot seal for the bascule pier, and it required a continuous flow of concrete for about 36 hours. The seal for several of the smaller supports [bents] followed. So it wasn't surprising that the tramway and concrete plant were lit up each night during this operation.

Of the 12 bents on the Glenada side, the two closest to the bank were located in tideland and had a rock, not sand, base. Since no footing was needed, no piling would be needed to be driven on these. Three more bents uphill would not be affected by tides and simply would need concrete bases — no coffer-dams, no piling. The seven other bents, often standing in water, would each need a cofferdam supported by piling.

The big pile driver's steam hammer, which had been a daily accompaniment to the folks of Glenada, suddenly stopped mid-December when it broke down. The older, slower drop hammer type of pile driver replaced it.

"While the steam hammer makes time with about a lick a second, the old-style pile driver does good work at one lick in five seconds. But the latter is said to produce a more finished product," explained the *Oar*. "In other words, it drives the piling to a greater depth."

#60
10-21-35

That was important, especially when it came to the main piers in the center of the river. Driving piling for the foot-ing of one of these was a very exacting job. "An inspector notes the rebound to every whack that the three-ton ham-mer gives. When the 78-foot piling re-fuses to go down more than a speck of an inch with 20 or 30 blows, he calls it a day for that piling and another is ordered right at its side with the same process. And so on and on until the whole cofferdam is filled with Siuslaw firs pounded to a depth of 30 or 40 feet below the bed of the river," explained an article in the *Oar* in December.

Preparing the forms for one of the two largest piers — a bascule pier —

Whoops!
On the Florence side, a steam donkey engine fell into the tied-arch pier coffer-dam before the water had been pumped out. Workers had to scramble to retrieve it before it fell in deeper.

from which one of the lift spans would swing was the most complex of the foundation work. Workmen were enclosed below water level in the cofferdam where large pumps kept leakage cleared. Several sections

Bascule Pier Rising Up

The solid concrete base of the Glenada side bascule pier shows with its timber cofferdam removed (at least the top 10 feet or so). Notice the structural and reinforcing steel (rebar) rising up that will be part of the massive pier.

were being built, upon the solid concrete seal. One of those was the form for the counterweight, which would counterbalance the lift. By the end of February, some of the steel reinforcing bars for the bascule pier were sticking up above the formwork — visible above water level.

Wherever a workman dumped heavy concrete from a wheelbarrow, another workman would be manning a concrete vibrator within the area where the concrete was being poured. This created a more even distribution.

The most serious accident to that point in the construction of the bridge occurred at the bascule pier on February 27, when worker Paul Grell slipped and fell into the large cofferdam. He was one of a number of wheelbarrow men dumping concrete into forms that day. He fell 10 to 15 feet, landing on his left shoulder. First-aid was provided by a local doctor; then he was hurried to Eugene, where surgery was required.

Work continued through January and February, driving piling and pouring seals on some bents and building the scaffolding and forms for the remaining piers and bents. By March 1, the last piling had been driven and the last cofferdam seal poured on all supports on the Glenada side. The next day, the big pile driver was moved to the Florence side where a number of cofferdams were ready.

Now the work of pouring piers and bents really got serious, and the trucks bringing cement from the railroad cars in Cushman to the concrete mixing plant were on the road continuously.

On March 22, the *Oar* reported that, while pouring concrete into the forms on the bascule pier, the cofferdam began to leak. Diver Zimmerman, called to the rescue, solved the problem by placing canvas on the cofferdam's exterior.

"While building the foundation on the Glenada side, a hoisting rig tipped and dropped a 10-inch pump and engine into the river on March 27. The hoisting rig had previously been on a barge, but had been moved to the falsework," reported the *Oar*. Even with the occasional accident and periods of bad weather, construction work was within a few days of being on schedule by the end of March.

By April 18, all the cofferdams used to construct the bents had been removed. And on May 10, the *Oar* reported, "Eight piers have been uncovered." In other words the forms also have been removed from that many bents. Even though the newly exposed Gothic-style arches looked more graceful than strong, they had the strength of more massive structures built in times past due to improvements in reinforced-concrete construction.

The *Oar* went on to say, "In the work so far, it is said that every pier [and bent] checks to the dot. This is complimentary to the carpenters as well as the engineers."

Finishing on Florence side

Starting in November 1934, the long, slow, back-breaking work of sinking cofferdams in the tidal flats began. On the north side of the river six of the bents were located above tidewater and the excavation, except for a few days when a team of horses and a scrapper were employed, was done by hand, using shovel and sledge. Five of these required two small cofferdams apiece spaced about a dozen feet apart. These 10 cofferdams needed to be 8 to 12 feet deep with heavy wood sheeting. Just like most of the other cofferdams, they needed piling that would be driven as deep as a steam hammer could drive them. And the piling would be packed in as close together as possible. Then they would be cut off near the bottom of the excavations without a concrete seal being poured, since these bents were not standing in deep water.

By April 26, 1935, at least 120 men were employed on the bridge and that didn't count the subcontractor jobs.

The first pouring of concrete on the Florence side took place May 10. Since the concrete plant was on the Glenada side, trucks hauling concrete had to come across on the ferry. After debarking, the trucks dumped their loads from an incline.

Throughout much of June, "the pile driver pounded away on the northern bascule pier, filling the cofferdam to the choking point with select piling," reported the *Oar*.

Watch Your Step

Between the partially completed sections and the piles of wood and rebar, you had to look around before taking a step.

Getting concrete to the Florence side was always a problem, but especially so when it was a large, continuous pour like the six-foot seal on the northern bascule pier that could not be interrupted once it began.

How to keep the concrete slush coming across the river continuously without disturbing the ferry service or sea-going commerce was the problem, and it was finally solved by using two derricks. Where the tramway ended on the Glenada side, one derrick would hoist a full yard of concrete — tramcar and all — onto a scow that moved over to the Florence side where a derrick would pick up the tramcar and dump the concrete slush through a big funnel. Two tramcars filled with concrete were taken in each scow load. By starting early in the mornings and working late, the job was completed.

By July 26, the second bascule pier had been pumped out and the piling sawed off a foot above the concrete seal. Carpenters then started building the forms within the big hole of the cofferdam.

Throughout August and into September work continued on the bascule pier, the tied arch pier, and the last couple of bents. By early September the last piling had been driven in the last cofferdam on the bridge. The end of the foundation work was in sight.

The Florence side had its share of accidents also. On October 21, a steam donkey engine fell into the tied-arch pier cofferdam before the water had been pumped out. Because the water level wasn't far from the engine, workers scrambled to retrieve it before it fell in deeper.

The late Goodren Gallo, a Florence old-timer, had her own cofferdam story. "My father, Olaf K. 'O.K.' Folvig was in charge of a group of men, one of whom was Howard Barrett of the pioneer Barrett family. While they were working in one of the supports [cofferdams], pumping out the water, my mother had a premonition. She didn't know exactly what my dad was doing on the bridge, but one night she awakened from a dream and said to him, 'Run, Olaf, run!' And he, half asleep, asked, 'Run where?' The next day, her dream stayed on his mind. Later, while working in the cofferdam, Olaf heard a strange pishing sound and knew this was the time to run. He told Barrett to jump out and run and he was right behind him. Immediately after, the cofferdam caved in. If they hadn't gotten out when they did, they could have been trapped and drowned."

By the end of September, the last of the cofferdams had been pumped out, all the piling had been sawed off within a few feet of the concrete seals, and wooden forms made to hold the concrete piers. At this point, the Florence side looked like a huge wooden maze. It was hard to see through the wood to the reinforced concrete supports being built. But on the Glenada side, with much of the wooden supports stripped away, it was easy to see the new, white concrete supports.

Inside a Pier

Workers place walls up to the pit floor in the Florence side bascule pier.

Glenada Bridge

Through the falsework notice two bents and the forms for the span they will be supporting. And above it all are the beginnings of the road deck.

CHAPTER 3

≈≈≈

The Superstructure

A BRIDGE'S SUPERSTRUCTURE is the horizontal portion that carries the traffic and spans between the supports and whatever rises above the road deck. When this part of the structure becomes visible, that's when it starts to really look like a bridge. The Siuslaw River Bridge, although considered one bridge, is technically two bridges that meet in the middle of the navigation channel. They were even built as two bridges. The Glenada Bridge had the temporary work bridge built before the Florence Bridge did. And Glenada was first to have the foundations and supports. When it came to the superstructure, it was the same story.

Throughout the construction process on both bridges, inspectors were amazed over and over again at the precision workmanship. So no one was surprised nearing the end of construction when the two bascule leaves met exactly where they were supposed to — well, almost. They were actually 1/72nd of an inch off, according to the *Portland Journal* from the 1 3/8 inch factored into the building specs as the distance between the two bascules when in the lowered position. That was simply another example of the precision that had become the hallmark of the Siuslaw River Bridge project. That's not to say there weren't any mistakes or accidents along the way, because there were. But the end re-

sults were consistently right on.

That's one of the reasons the Siuslaw River Bridge was chosen by Judith Dupre to be included in *Bridges: A History of the World's Most Famous and Important Spans*. It represented so well McCullough's technical genius in bridge building. Another reason was that this bridge also represented his aesthetic genius. This bridge over the Siuslaw River not only showcased McCullough's trademark Art Deco and Moderne embellishments, but it also celebrated the stylized Egyptian sunburst motif in the domed pier houses and on the entry pylons as well as the Gothic influence on the arch supports and bracketed balustrades. This variety of decoration is not seen in most of his bridges.

The Glenada Bridge

By the end of March 1935, the maze of wood reaching higher and higher was a dead giveaway that the superstructure was under way. And if people thought the bridge was being built of wood, it was perfectly understandable. At this point, much of it was. However, all that wood was falsework, providing temporary support and forms for the concrete. It would later be removed. About this time the *Oar* commented, "The carpenters are having their inning

Passing Inspection?

Sidewalks are being readied for concrete pour on the Glenada Bridge. Notice tramcars in the distance in front of the tied arch — a work in progress.

in the construction with this vast amount of falsework, every bit of which must be placed to the fraction of an inch."

With many of the bridge supports finished and the vast amounts of wooden deck girder falsework in place, it wasn't long before the deck girders were poured. They would provide the underpinning of the road deck of the south viaduct. And by mid-April, finish work on the road deck surface began. The road deck's reinforced concrete surface had to be screeded — leveled and smoothed — after it was poured. The screed apparatus looked like connected, movable roof trusses. Ray Bottenberg in *Bridges of the Oregon Coast* explained that the apparatus held a timber that workers moved back and forth working the concrete to establish a flat surface at the required height.

All along the Glenada Bridge, work was progressing nicely. "Concrete pouring, frame building, everything clicks with the nicest precision," stated the *Oar* at the end of May.

In mid-July, the reinforced concrete tied arch was poured. And by mid-August, the arch's falsework below the road deck was removed and this "bowstring" arch was completed. Polishing of the concrete had begun by the end of August and would continue from now until the bridge was completed.

The rattle of hammers driving rivets in September meant that the steel bascule lift span was being assembled. It would gradually arch toward Florence as it headed northward from the big pier.

At the same time, more road deck work took place on the tied arch. The sidewalks were poured with the structural steel extending upwards for the future balustrade posts (balusters) as well as for the hangers that would provide support between the deck and the arch ribs.

By the end of October, the reinforced-concrete deck girder spans — all 12 of them — appeared almost finished with much of the bracketed balustrades completed. The tied arch, while looking finished, still had some of its above deck falsework and the steel bascule span was now in place. Below the road deck, the bents with their Gothic-style arches supporting much of the superstructure were totally finished with no scaffolding or forms showing except the temporary work bridges, and they were gone by November.

There were few accidents during the construction of the bridge and some were probably not reported. Gallo told about one that no doubt fell into that category: "One of the workers, Nester Barnhardt, missed his footing one day and fell into the river," she said, suppressing a chuckle. "He had been in the Coast Guard, I think, and must have been a strong swimmer because he made it to shore while holding a pack of cigarettes up out of the water. He was sure proud of that."

The late Ed Tatum, a bridge worker who also had a potentially life-threatening accident, most likely didn't report his fall either. "One morning while I was working on the bridge, I fell into the river," he told Dick Smith in 1986. "I was able to swim to the Glenada side and catch the ferry to Florence. Then I went home, changed my clothes, and went back to work. That was the Depression, and I wanted to keep my job."

Prior to his being a worker on the bridge, he had been a security guard on it from 4 p.m. until late at night. After it got dark each night, his wife, Alma, would bring dinner out on the partially built bridge and stay to eat and walk back and forth with him for a while.

Laborers earned between 50 cents and $1.50 an hour. According to the *Oar*, "A family of five (two adults and three children ages 3 to 12) could live nicely on a food budget of $4.56 per

Not a Wood Bridge?

All of this wood is temporary falsework that will be tossed in the river when no longer needed. Notice the emerging bascule pier at the end of the Glenada Bridge. Also, notice the truck at the ferry landing.

Coming Together

The nearly finished Glenada Bridge joins the still-under-construction Florence Bridge.

week." The pay was low, but it gave people jobs and hope for the future.

The Florence Bridge

By September, the main action had moved to the Florence side. As the September 6 issue of the *Oar* stated, "Now they are building a bridge on the Florence side of the river to connect with the Glenada Bridge." And Mercer–Fraser's Superintendent Acheson assured the townsfolk that Front Street [Bay Street] traffic would not be impaired.

Even though both bridges were being built of reinforced concrete and steel, as much lumber was used in the construction process as if the bridges had been built of wood. Many of the timbers used were up to 40 or 50 feet long. Andy Nordahl, who was a kid then and lived along the river, remembered how it looked. "The ferry route took us under the bridge while it was being built, because it went from the Florence landing on the east side of the bridge to west of the bridge on the Glenada side. It was amazing to see all the lumber they used for the forms and scaffolding." He was able to get a really good look.

As those forms and scaffolding were no longer needed, the wood was simply dropped in the river nails and all — definitely not in compliance with today's Occupational Safety and Health Administration (OSHA) rules. Much of the wood washed ashore downriver and upriver; people collected it and either used it or sold it. Collecting bridge wood provided a means of income for those out of work and for kids.

"We lived on Duncan Island about 6 miles upriver," remembers Fred Jensen. "For us kids, the bridge supplied the materials to build our playhouse. We just couldn't wait to get out in the morning to walk up the riverbank or to take a rowboat out to see what the tides had brought us that night. There would be two inchers and one-inch lumber and we'd pick 'em up and take 'em home. We'd pick the nails out and straighten 'em. That was our supply of nails. It might take several days for the wood to make its way that far upriver, but eventually, we had enough to make a good-sized playhouse." And others salvaged enough to build even larger houses.

Paul Weber had been on the job of delivering reinforcing steel, mostly from Portland, since the bridge job began. Lengths up to 50 feet were not uncommon and night runs were often necessary to keep workmen on the job. "Paul contrived an appliance, which led the trailer wheels, over 30 feet back of the truck proper, to follow in the truck's track. In going around curves, this was not only a time saver but counted for safety too," reported the *Oar* on October 25, 1935. "Two more truckloads of steel will end the deliveries for the Siuslaw River Bridge."

A week later, the paper reported on a big day for workmen pouring concrete. "Two eight-hour shifts were spent pouring concrete for the girder beams on a good-sized section of the north end. The material was mixed at the Glenada plant and brought over by the ferry in trucks and transferred to wheel carts at the extreme north end of the bridge. Over 230 cubic yards were poured."

On November 22, the newspaper announced that the following Sunday those who were careful may walk across the Siuslaw "dryshod." That didn't mean the road deck was totally paved, because it wasn't. Part of it was falsework. And except for that Sunday, the public was not allowed to walk on either bridge. The first to accomplish this feat was credited to George Wilbur. But rumors abounded of others who claimed to be first — crossing when no workers were around.

Unique Pier Houses

The two pier houses on the Florence side are under construction. Notice the steel railing in place on the lift span.

Pier House Up Close

Work goes on inside and out.

Later that winter, Gallo and a friend had quite an adventure crossing the bridge. "It was during my senior year of high school that the bridge was being built," she explained, "and I was on the girls' basketball team — the center. One night we were away to a game and got back after the ferry quit running, which was after midnight. The Florence Hotel would let people sleep in the lobby if they missed the ferry, but my friend — who lived near me in Glenada — and I didn't want to sleep in the hotel lobby. We wanted to go home. So we decided to cross the bridge. Of course, it wasn't finished. Only the workers were allowed on it, but we did it anyway. We were teenagers. And we discovered that the walkway over some of the river was only a couple planks wide with no side supports. I don't know how we made it. It was so dark, we could barely see where we were going."

By the end of December, it was possible for anyone to walk across the bridge, if they first requested permission, because the remaining deck girders were poured and most of the falsework removed.

Then the remaining tied arch was poured early in 1936, which was the last big concrete pour to take place. Throughout January, minor pours continued for cross braces, but the days were numbered for the concrete mixing plant.

"The polishing job of the concrete goes on just before the wrecking of the falsework. And the polishing job is intricate," reported the *Oar*. "The bridge must look pretty from every angle when it is done. The boys who do this work are by no means idle hands." Every visible part of the concrete was rubbed smooth with Carborundum abrasive to eliminate any imperfections caused by the wooden forms.

Although the construction project continued moving along smoothly, a couple of bridge related mishaps occurred in the winter of 1936. On January 13, the Florence Bridge survived a flood, during which a heavy accumulation of drift collected against the tied arch's falsework, but, fortunately, no damage was done.

The tug *May*, used to move barges as needed for the bridge-building project, was tied up at a dock at Florence where it caught fire one night early in 1936 and was badly damaged. According to Jensen, owner Trygve Nordahl salvaged the motor and then it was pushed downriver, just like with the bridge wood and a lot of the trash in those days.

By the end of January 1936, approximately 95 workers were busy from one end of the Florence Bridge to the other and a few on the Glenada Bridge too. Their work included welding and riveting of the steel handrail on both sides of the steel bascule span. Also, at this time, a carpenter crew began on the pier houses on the Florence Bridge. The two on the Glenada Bridge were already begun.

With the steel handrail in place on both the Glenada Bridge and Florence Bridge, it looked like one long connected handrail. And when the two steel bascule spans were completed and there was no longer a gap between them, they looked like one connected arch. It was hard to think of two bridges anymore. They had become one.

The Siuslaw River Bridge

By the end of the first week in February, the pouring of the bracketed balustrades on the northern viaduct was completed. During the rest of the month, crews built forms for the northern pier houses and poured the southern pier houses, painters finished applying green paint to the steel bascule spans, and concrete finishers continued the endless job of smoothing the concrete with the Carborundum. By the end of the month, the pier houses all had their domed look and the bascule piers had electricity installed. To the workers, the end was in sight.

Each week fewer men were needed. The year started with more than a hundred weekly average, and by March it was down to 65. It wasn't hard to see that the job was winding down; some of the construction buildings on the Glenada side had already been torn down.

The bridge was beginning to have a finished look. The entire road deck, which measured 27 feet wide, was completed, and sidewalks, measuring 3 1/2 feet wide on each side of the road, were poured in early March. That was the last pouring of concrete for the entire bridge. The grinding noise of the mixing plant was finally silenced — much to the delight of Glenada residents.

Contracts for the approach grading were open to bid on March 5. This would not be a big job because the bridge approaches had long since been completed, including paving. All that would be necessary would be to connect them to the bridge. This would involve short distances on each end of the bridge, requiring filling, grading, baserock, and paving.

Traffic lights were installed. And "on each arch, there will be a beacon light in two colors," reported the *Oar* on March 13. "These will signify by their lights that the plane is over the Siuslaw Bridge. From this the aviator can take his bearing."

A crew of about 40 took on the finish-up tasks. Electrical machinery was installed in the bascule spans. The balance of the riprap was placed around the foundations of both bascule piers. Glaziers put glass in each of the four pier house windows. And concrete finishers continued working from one end of the bridge to the other. It wouldn't be long; the bridge would open to traffic as soon as surfacing was in place on the northern approach fill.

The bridge actually opened to traffic March 31 at 12:45. Yet, that didn't stop the concrete finishers; they continued on.

An average crew of 30 did general clean up, made more adjustments to machinery in the bascules, and at long last completed the concrete finishing. Final inspection occurred on April 9 and 10 and the Siuslaw River Bridge was announced complete on April 10. Those concrete finishers must have done a fantastic job, because several references referred to how "white" and sparkling and beautiful the new bridge looked.

Innovative Tied Arch Bridge Design

TIED ARCHES, used in many McCullough bridges, were one of his most successful innovations. In a tied arch, the outward-directed horizontal forces that try to flatten the arch are redirected and become compression, squeezing the bridge together. This is done by making the arch and the bottom chord (either the road deck or tie rods) one integrated structure, like an archery bow and string. Hence the alternate name "bowstring" arch. The bottom chord, which represents the string, holds the arch, which represents the bow, in compression. Because of this type of construction, the superstructure is able to rest on piers that are light weight, not massive.

Having one integrated structure was also the theory behind James Marsh's "rainbow arch" that Mc-Cullough learned about early in his career. McCullough took Marsh's idea and improved on it by using more efficient reinforcing steel instead of steel plate and latticework and using

hinges (rotation points) near the top of each arch rib to simplify construction. He used tied arches on several of the coastal bridges, either where he couldn't have massive supports or didn't want massive supports.

Where the Tied Arch Ties

The structural steel bottom chord connects with the reinforced concrete arch.

Concrete seems so solid and we can't imagine it moving without cracking, but it can move and this must be allowed for during construction. The problem of movement in the integrated tied arch was solved by use of rollers on each side of the road deck of one end of the arch. "The rollers are part of a bearing device that supports one end of the tied arch while allowing for thermal expansion and contraction," explained David Johnson ODOT lead electrical engineer.

In 1999, when the periodical *ENR* listed McCullough among the top 10 bridge engineers, Hadlow noted, "The periodical cited McCullough's use of the reinforced-concrete tied arch as his most innovative contribution."

Precision Bascule Lift

THE SIUSLAW RIVER BRIDGE has a double leaf bascule, which means twin lift spans tilt away from each other when raised and reconnect end to end when lowered. Bascule means seesaw in French and a seesaw or teeter-totter is a good way to describe how it works. As the road deck portion of the bascule lifts, the unseen counterweight lowers farther into the main pier. It swings sideways and down into the bascule pit — an area as large as a banquet room. This area must be kept absolutely clear. Anything in the way will either be crushed or, if large enough, halt the opening of the bridge and possibly cause damage. There's a ladder along the wall for access because occasionally things do fall in the pit.

The counterweights move simultaneously on both sides. These are large, room-size hunks of solid concrete, and they are permanent. Each of these have side openings that hold stacks of various weights. "The bridge is checked for balance every so often," explained ODOT Inspector Nate Neal, "and, when necessary, weights are added or removed." From a casual glance, you would think these side openings were simply storage areas.

According to David Johnson, ODOT lead electrical engineer, "There are two principles that make a bascule bridge work — balance and using gears to greatly multiply force. The best way to explain balance is to make the analogy to a simple teeter-totter. It is possible for a small child to perfectly balance a large adult on such a teeter-totter by having the adult sit in close

The Trunnion

Each bascule pier has one trunnion on a 14-inch axle supported by two bearings.

to the balance bar in the middle and have the child sit as far as possible at the other end. In the case of the bridge, the large counterweight, like the adult, is placed very close to the balance point, and the movable span, like the small child, is placed far away from the balance point. A trunnion is the balance point and grease is pumped into it so that it is easy to turn." Each end of the bridge has one trunnion on a 14-inch axle supported by two bearings — one on each end of the axle shaft.

"With regard to using gears to increase force," continued Johnson, "using a car jack to change a flat tire demonstrates that. A person cannot lift a car all by themself, but they can with the help of a car jack. Each of the two 15-horsepower electric motors cannot generate the thousands of pounds of force necessary to raise and lower the movable bridge by turning the trunnion, but in combination with gears, they can."

All operations are controlled from the pier houses that are built over the corners of the piers — totally out of the way of the road deck. It only takes a couple of minutes for the siren to blare, gates descend, and the bridge lift, and the same amount of time to lower the bridge spans and raise the gates.

Safety measures are built in. Before the pins locking the two leaves together can be drawn, the roadway gates must be down. This sequence is reversed in closing. The gates cannot be raised until the leaves are closed and the locking pins in place.

Bascule Span in Action

This double leaf bascule design depends on each side working simultaneously.

Walt Fossek, a long-time Florence commercial fisherman,

likes to tell of the time he somehow didn't notice the light turn red or the sirens blare and got stuck between the gates and the rising bridge. He said the gate came down behind him and he couldn't back up and then the wall of rising road deck in front of him made it difficult to go anywhere. He said he was mighty scared, especially when he saw that the lead car on the other side was a police car. He thought for sure he would get a ticket — but he didn't.

Even though the pier houses were built with the intention of having a full-time bridge tender, that never actually happened. Today, boats must give ODOT two hours notice for when they want the bridge open because the tender who handles the Siuslaw River Bridge is stationed several miles from Florence.

The bascule span has been raised and lowered over and over during its 75-year history with a near perfect record of precision openings and closings. Then during 2009–2010, it had a total makeover that will certainly ease its way into the future.

CHAPTER 4

~~~~~

Low-Key Opening & Big-Time Dedication

As the bridge neared completion in the spring of 1936, Florence braced for an onslaught of newcomers and visitors.

Removal of construction offices and various temporary buildings, primarily located on the Glenada side, continued through March. As to the incredible amount of wooden falsework used on and around the bridge during construction, only a small amount remained under the northern tied arch by the end of March. And that was gone prior to the opening.

The *Oar* reported that all bids were rejected for doing the final fill work and other improvements at the two ends of the new bridge, so the work ended up being done by a highway maintenance crew of five or six men under the direction of Guy Faris. And they had only 10 days to get it done before the bridge opened to traffic. The bulldozer employed on the northern bridge approach finished moving the last of the fill the day before the bridge opened.

And, according to the *Portland Journal*, with only hours left before opening to traffic, the two sides of the bascule span were raised so that the counterweights could be carefully adjusted.

On-time, no-frills opening

The Siuslaw River Bridge opened to the public Tuesday, March 31, 1936, only 20 months after the start of construction in August 1934. "School was dismissed and children took part in the parade on bicycles," according to the *Port Umpqua Courier.*

"I remember when they first opened the bridge," said Andy Nordahl, quoted in the *Siuslaw News.* "We lived in Glenada, and the cars were lined up on both sides of the river waiting to cross. They cut the ribbon. Then the cars drove over."

Promptly at 12:45 p.m., approximately 100 cars moved slowly across the new bridge followed by the children and then doubled back again. "The parade was headed by [Florence] Mayor George P. Edwards, followed by Cal Young, county commissioner, P.M. Morse, county engineer, Earl Hill, state representative, and reporters from both Eugene papers and several Portland papers," reported the *Oar.* "The parade began and ended without one word of speechmaking or one blast of music, yet in it all there was the finest display of smiling goodwill."

Opening Day

March 31, 1936, opening day saw approximately 100 cars parade across the bridge and back. At the time the bridge opened, the ferry Tourist I *stopped running.*

And the air was filled with all kinds of celebratory noise making: sirens and whistles, church bells, horns, and loud cheering.

The late Don Bowman, Florence resident and former mayor, was 5 years old when it opened, "I remember going across the bridge with my parents and then turning around and going right back over."

The state highway department ordered the ferry service between Florence and Glenada stopped simultaneous with the barriers on each end of the bridge being lifted. This bridge opening marked the first of the five bridges of the Coast Bridges Project to be completed and opened for travel.

With no ferry to wait for, cars began wheeling over the bridge with nothing to stop them. The chamber of commerce was glad to see that cars coming from the south nearly all made the sharp turn down into Florence's business district.

"Cars from Minnesota, Florida, Texas, South Dakota, and California were among those to make the first trip across the bridge. Ten minutes after the bridge opened, a car from Wisconsin rolled across, indicating how advanced the tourist season was even at this early date," reported the *Corvallis Gazette-Times*.

The *Oar*'s editor, M.D. Morgan, gave vent to his feelings about traveling across the bridge about a month after it opened. "Without doubt, thousands of people in their autos flit by the Washington monument every day. But when it comes to the Siuslaw Bridge — one of the most beautiful structures in all America — it gives us pleasure to note the number of cars that pass along slowly to admire its beauty. . . . And we excuse those who are on a mission of mercy. But how anyone with a desire to view the betterment of a great state can flit across such a bridge without slowing to moderate speed gets our goat."

The speed limit as set by the State Highway Commission on the bridge was 25 miles per hour and, according to Editor Morgan, "That's too fast."

Double whammy planning

Florence began rounding out its plans for dedication ceremonies to be held in conjunction with the annual rhododendron festival months before the bridge opened for traffic. Local folks became interested as they realized that it would be one of the largest celebrations to ever take place in their town. "Dedicating a half-million-dollar improvement is not a common occasion in a town the size of Florence," reported the *Oar* on January 17. The population of Florence was approximately 350 at the time.

Representatives from fraternal and other local organizations, the Grange, and the city's business community all pledged their support at a March meeting of the Siuslaw Chamber of Commerce. At the same meeting, a Portland news story generated a certain amount of ire because it stated that Marshfield [Coos Bay] wanted its bridge dedication and Florence's merged, since the two were being held two weeks apart. According to the *Oar*, "The local secretary was instructed to write the Coos Bay Bridge celebration promoters that any such idea was out of the question!"

Even though the event was being held in Florence, Eugene was not left out. Bob Fischer of Eugene was selected as promotion manager for the event, including the queen contest, which involved the sale of buttons. Approximately 5,000 buttons were expected to sell for 25 cents apiece.

The *Oar* announced that the first consignment of the two-color buttons bearing a picture of the new bridge arrived by mid-April and that the contest for queen was on. The newspaper also

Opening Day Parade

The cars and trucks paraded across and back accompanied by children on bicycles.

announced that the supply of celebration bumper strips was exhausted and 250 more would be ordered.

On April 24, a good-sized delegation of Florence residents left for Eugene to attend a chamber of commerce reception in honor of the queen candidates. No doubt, several buttons were sold that day.

With just weeks to go before the big event, plans were beginning to jell. The major portion of the combined observances was scheduled for Sunday morning, including the bridge dedication. "Following this," explained the *Oar*, "if the day be favored with sunshine, it is planned to close that portion of Front Street adjacent to the bridge for the celebrated seafood dinner at which the multitudes will be served."

The man who had been asked to be the principal speaker, former Governor A.W. Norblad, had accepted.

This was cause for celebration because he was not only a coastal resident and long-time proponent of the coast highway, but a well-known personage in the state.

During the last couple of weeks, the queen candidates were busy. Besides selling buttons and appearing at functions, they had some rather "unqueenly" competitions in which they had to participate. Each candidate had to show off her fishing and rowing talents, even though she wasn't running to be queen of water sports. A fishing contest was held at Westlake and a boat-rowing race held on Tahkenitch Lake.

But the most unusual event was the old automobile "race," where the slowest car would be the winner. Cars had to be at least 10 years old. The queen candidates rode along, but someone else did the driving in these pre-1927 cars. Think Model Ts (Model As would've been too new). As it turned out, only one car made it to the finish line; the others were disqualified because they couldn't quite make it. They quit running.

Only a week before the celebration, the *Oar* announced that invitations had been sent to all the chambers of commerce in the Willamette Valley and up and down the coast as well as to all state officials and newspapermen in Oregon. It seems the event promoters didn't want to leave anybody out.

Because a crowd of approximately 15,000 attended the dedication of the unfinished Alsea Bay Bridge in Waldport on May 8–10, expectations were high for a large crowd for the Siuslaw River Bridge Dedication and Rhododendron Days celebrations May 23–24.

Two-in-one festive celebration

With streets gaily decorated and a favorable weather forecast, Florence was ready for the two-day, two-event celebration and so was Gail Darling — the new Queen Rhododendra. She and her court of four princesses would reign over Rhododendron Days and the Siuslaw River Bridge Dedication.

The *Oar* reported, "Tables to accommodate 600 people at a time at the salmon feed, are to be ready Saturday morning. On Sunday, there will be fried salmon by Earl Smith (famed for his salmon fries along the coast), oceans of crab, ground clams, barrels of coffee, and gallons of cream. All the niceties."

And a collection of buttons, pictures, and souvenirs from past rhododendron day celebrations were on display in the store window in the Kyle Building. (Very similar to what is done today at the Siuslaw Pioneer Museum.)

Queen Rhododendra and her princesses began their reign Saturday evening at the coronation ceremony at the Florence Hotel. A concert by the Siuslaw High School band preceded the coronation and the queen's banquet followed. And a special guest attended — Flossie Huntington — who as Flossie Chapman was Queen Rhododendra in 1909.

The final event of the first night included dancing on the dock just off the foot of Front Street, with music furnished by the Standard Oil Company's sound car, which had huge megaphone-like speakers on top facing in all directions.

By 10 a.m. Sunday, a throng, estimated at anywhere from 6,000 to 10,000, gathered on the bridge or as close as they could get. During the dedication ceremony, they heard band music, listened to speeches, and watched Queen Rhododendra christen the bridge with a bottle of ginger ale. Even though Prohibition had ended, no one had the nerve to use champagne.

"The voice of the Standard Oil sound car kept the crowds in good humor," reported the *Oar*, "as did the peppy music of the four visiting bands — Eugene High School band, Cottage Grove Boy

Showing Off

The new Siuslaw River Bridge shows off its double-leaf bascule lift capability.

Siuslaw Bridge Dedication, Queen Janet at Home and Other Shots

Bridge Dedication

The Morning Oregonian *featured a photo spread on the dedication of the Siuslaw River Bridge on May 24, 1936. Queen Janet (right above and below) was the newly elected queen of Portland's upcoming rose festival.*

Scouts Drum and Bugle Corps, Corvallis American Legion Drum Corps, and the Oregon State Insurance band of Corvallis."

Governor C.H. Martin, who was scheduled to speak, was absent due to his wife being ill. Among the speakers was Mayor David Leeming of Victoria, British Columbia, who reminded everyone that there is nothing like completed international highways to develop brotherhood between nations.

A.W. Norblad of Astoria, formerly governor, state senator, and president of the Coast Highway Association delivered the principal address. He had been in the senate when Ben Jones introduced the first bill providing for construction of the coast route in 1919 and had worked toward that end ever since. In his speech, he made a comprehensive summary of the efforts entailed in building the highway and ended on a high note. "Completion of the Oregon Coast highway by the dedication of these new bridges," he proclaimed, "brings to successful fulfillment the dream of 17 years ago."

In the afternoon, rescue drills of the Coast Guard held the attention of those watching from the bridge and waterfront. And before and after the drills, the lift span of the new bridge raised and lowered, much to the delight of the multitudes.

Final Words

"When all five bridges were completed, the celebration was held in each of the towns [except for the Umpqua River Bridge] on different weekends, so that everyone could attend all of them if they wanted to," reminisced the late Goodren Gallo. "I remember that Florence was noted for its clams, and always had free chowder at the Rhody Festival. Well, there was free chowder at this celebration, all right."

Editor Morgan was so pleased with the bridge that a week after the dedication he offered these words of praise. "While all five of the coast's new wonderful bridges are the work of skilled engineers, the *Oar* wishes to compliment the men who designed the beautiful bridge here at Florence.

"It was a most technical piece of work," he went on. "Every piling had to be driven to the dot, and the sand and gravel was weighed as it was dumped in the hopper to mix with cement. Everything synchronized. The engineers and the builders worked in harmony. The job was done on time."

The ceremony included a eulogy to the late George M. Miller who had been a leading citizen of Florence and the town's most ardent promoter. He would have been thrilled beyond words with the new bridge.

Years later in 1997, the bridge still garnered high praise, "The Siuslaw River Bridge is a good example of his [McCullough's] eclectic structural and design vocabulary," wrote Judith Dupre in *Bridges: A History of the World's Most Famous and Important Spans*. "It is a movable bridge, a double-leaf bascule that is flanked by two tied concrete arches, each 154 feet long. The bridge and its approaches are enhanced with detailing and ornamentation — as seen in the pylons, bridge houses, bracketed balustrades, and approach arches — that reflect McCullough's masterly use of concrete and exuberant quotation of Art Deco, Egyptian, and Gothic motifs."

The Bridge

In commemoration of the Siuslaw River Bridge, Reverend R.H. Neff penned the following poem, which was published in *The Siuslaw Oar* on April 17, 1936:

Thou standeth in thy strength and beauty,
At thy feet the waters go softly,
Washing with the strength of mountains and the sea.

Thou hast in thee,
The heart and mind of man,
Bringing together far distant lands of great plains and
Golden sands.

There is in thee the echo of vineyards, the laughter of
The harvest-fields,
The lowing of flocks, the song of birds,
And the laughter of children.

Age finds delights and rest in thy beauty and strength.
Ships will pass through thee with wealth from far-off places
The work of strange and distant races.

Traffic shall wear its deep lines,
In the face of thy beaten road,
With many a wheel and the sterner tooth of time.

There is in thee something more than steel and
Molded stone,

There are the ideals of a nation,
The passions of a great people that shall speak to ages yet
To come.

The singer, the painter, and the speaker shall find in thee
A power
That shall quicken the heart, the tongue, the eye, and
The hand
In song and story of conquest and glory.

Through thy strong arches,
Perhaps an army marches,
With lumbering cannon, drum, and trumpets sounding.

Thou mayest yet be the bridge of sighs for a race and
People,
Or perhaps some distant wanderer may stop beside thy
Lonely and forsaken pathway,
To meditate upon the frailty of human endeavor.

Who knows what paeans of praise,
May sanctify the building of thy form here beside the sea;
But forever we shall rejoice in thee!

COAST GUARD DRILL

BEACH APPARATUS DRILL—

Imagine that the dredge out on the river is a ship in distress and the spar standing in the water stands 100 yards from shore, and represents the masts of a vessel requiring assistance from which it is desired to rescue any passengers or members of the crew wanting ashore. As you follow the drill you will notice that the officer in charge and the boatswain-mate are placing the Lyle-gun—this is a miniature cannon—in position for firing. One man is providing a shot, another the shot line. The officer in charge then inserts a two-ounce bag of black powder in the bore of the gun. The shot is now placed to which the line has been bent. The shot weighs 18 pounds; the length of the shot-line in today's drill is 2200 feet. A sand anchor is buried which will serve as an anchorage for the howser the farthest end of which will be attached to the spar. A block and tackle is used to tighten all the slack in the line. The breeches buoy (a large pair of canvass trousers) is attached to a cork life buoy and hauled to the spar. The man on shore stretch a "cats-paw" and hook it to the block of the sand anchor. The crew manning the whip line haul the breeches buoy to the supposed ship wreck. The crew then moves to the whip line on the opposite side and hauls the passengers ashor.

CAPSIZE DRILL—

This drill will be performed with the pulling life-boat. This boat is self bailing. The boat contains air tanks in eight separate compartments. The bilges are water-tight. The boat is purposely capsized today by all members of the crew moving to one side and leaning backwards. By means of righting lines the crew again leans back, all members on one side. As the boat rights itself the crew re-enters the boat; the water running out of the scuppers. This demonstrates how a boat would actually be righted after it has been capsized by heavy seas.

BOAT PULLING DRILL—

The Coast Guard will now show how to use the "pulling surf boat." This type of rescue is used in shallow water of the ocean and beach on or near spits, or in shoalwater. A coxswain is in charge with a crew of six men, each at an oar. As nearly as possible this demonstration will show how this boat can ride a heavy sea. Good headway will be given; crew will face about and hold and exert full power in checking headway; demonstrate how boat can be instantly stopped in rescue work, draw away from shoals or dangerous objects or in avoiding breakers.

Siuslaw Bridge Dedication

and

Annual Rhododendron Festival

May 23-24, 1936

FLORENCE, OREGON

EXECUTIVE COMMITTEE

Earl Hill - - - - - - - - General Chairman
W. J. Kyle - - - - - - - - Finance Chairman
A. E. Neilson - - - - - - - - - Treasurer
Lee Griner - - - - - - - - - - Publicity
Gilbert Houghton - - - - - - Entertainment
Dr. G. P. Edwards - - - - - - - Housing
George Carle - - - - - - - Seafood Dinner
Leslie Swarthout - - - - - - - Reception
John Blaylock - - - - - - - Concessions
Robert M. Fischer Jr. - - - - - - Manager

Queen Rhododendron VIII Court

Miss Gail Darling - - - - - **Queen**
Miss Vernice Redifer - - - - **Princess**
Miss Charlene Fernald - - - - **Princess**
Miss Ruth Haring - - - - **Princess**
Miss Grace Boak - - - - **Princess**

Gowns worn by queens from McMorran and Washburne Store
Flowers furnished by University Florist, Eugene.

PROGRAM

SATURDAY, MAY 23

6:00 p. m. — Queen Rhododendron's Banquet, Florence Hotel.

7:30 p. m. — Concert by band, on West Main street.

8:00 p. m. — Coronation ceremonies for Queen Rhododendron, West Main street.

9:00 p. m. — Queen Rhododendron's Ball, Liberty Hall.

SUNDAY, MAY 24

10:00 a. m. — Band Concert by Eugene High School band.

10:30 a. m. — Dedication ceremonies, on the new bridge.

Address of welcome by Mayor G. P. Edwards, Florence.

Introduction of distinguished guests by Earl Hill, general chairman.

Eulogy to George Melvin Miller by Cal M. Young.

Address by Governor Charles H. Martin.

Christening of bridge by Queen Rhododendron.

Dedication address, Former Governor A. W. Norblad, of Astoria.

12:00 noon — Annual Seafood Dinner, West Main street, near bridge.

1:30 p. m. — Corvallis Drum Corps program, West Main street.

2:00 p. m. — Opening of Bridge Draw.

Coast Guard drill and demonstration.

3:00 p. m. — Baseball game.

Afternoon dancing.

Plaques Make It Official

Plaques on the northeast entry pylon of the Siuslaw River Bridge recognize the Mercer-Fraser Company as its contractor and notes that it was a project of the Federal Emergency Administration of Public Works completed in 1936.

PART II

POST CONSTRUCTION

~~~~~

CHAPTER 5

Impacts on Glenada & Florence

THE COMPLETION of the Siuslaw River Bridge greatly changed the futures of both Glenada and Florence. Glenada's town gradually dwindled away as businesses moved across the river, and the northern bridge approach created another location for Florence businesses along the new stretch of the Oregon Coast Highway. The move was gradual, but it was the beginning of the end of the waterfront as the center of town and the beginning of the business strip along the highway . . . for both towns.

Although Florence boasted a larger population than Glenada in 1936, it wasn't always that way. Around the turn of the 20th century Glenada was the larger of the two towns.

Glenada's Past

"Early on, there were a lot of buildings and stores down on the waterfront over there," remembered Fred Jensen.

Edna Miles, writing in the Siuslaw Pioneer Museum's Pioneer Series in 1970, says that when she arrived in town as a young teacher in the fall of 1914, "Glenada was an incorporated town and quite a business center. The main thoroughfare was a wide plank road, running from the ferry landing along the river nearly to Maple Street [close to Pritchard Park]. Many business houses and two saloons flanked the boardwalk. Local option had been voted in that year and Glenada became quite a gathering place for the many railroad men who were in the area at the time."

Miles even remembered the names of early businesses. "Some of the business houses were Sam Bigg's Blacksmith Shop, N.B. Hull Hardware, Bob Lowe's Grocery Store, Frank Knowles' General Store, the city hall, the post office (in Bob Lowe's store, with Lowe the first postmaster), the two saloons, a sawmill, Grandpa Johnson's Shop (where he made boats, furniture, and coffins for the local people), and Flint's Livery Stable up the hill from the end of the boardwalk."

At the top of the hill stood the Hotel Glenada, which was a gathering place for town events — especially school events for many years. Then the old hotel was replaced by the Blue Roof Motel, and years later in the early 1970s the Pier Point Inn was built there. Miles remembered them all.

In April 1930, Glenada's ferry approach, where cars drove

Glenada's Downtown

Cars drive the plank road along Glenada's waterfront in the 1920s. At the turn of the 20th century, Glenada had been larger than Florence.

down to get on the ferry, was only able to hold a few cars. So the State Highway Commission made sure Glenada received a new one that could handle more cars. As the highway neared completion, traffic increased. The new ferry approach was greatly appreciated.

The completion of the bridge in 1936 was not good news for the business community of Glenada. Little by little, the businesses moved to Florence or just quit operating. And before long, Glenada lost its post office.

"But what Glenada lost as a business town," said Miles, "she gained as a residential area." New roads were built and the town spread with residences throughout the hills and new businesses along the highway.

Ferry farewell

While the bridge wasn't such a good deal for Glenada's business community, it put the kibosh on the ferry and ferrymen. The ferry was no longer needed, and the ferrymen were out of work. It had been a major part of the life of both towns. And for many tourists, it was a pleasant diversion on a long road trip.

"The story of Grant L. Colter, who for 25 years carried folks back and forth across the Siuslaw River, the first of the five ferries to be discontinued through completion of a bridge, is almost the story of ferry development and final disappearance on the coast," wrote Harold Say with the Oregon State Highway Commission in *The Oregon Motorist*.

"First, he crossed with rowboats, then came a barge-and-tug operation, finally the modern diesel propelled ferry. He is another ferryman with a 'no accident' record."

Say, in the same article, quoted Marian Lowry writing in Eugene's *Register–Guard* who spoke for locals as well as tourists:

A half dozen times we crossed with him [Colter] getting his recollections bit by bit as he talked in the intervals when he was not busy. And we shared something of his wistfulness and sadness, because we too shall miss the ferry — the rattle of the approach boards, the clank of the heavy chains, the swish of the water, the chug-chug of the engine and the privilege to view leisurely the scenery about the curving river, the sand dunes stretching away to the west, the timbered ridges to the east. Folks who go racing over the bridge will have little time to enjoy all this.

Capricious tides

After the burned-out tug, the *May*, had been pushed down-river "to get rid of it," the tide didn't cooperate. It propelled the *May* back upriver, and Jensen's uncle, Lorence Jensen, saw it, snagged it, and tied it to his dock.

"That was 1936, just about the time Uncle Lorence was considering applying for the mail route between Mapleton and Cushman," recalled Jensen. "And Granddad Mads Jensen, being a good boat builder, overhauled the burned-out tug with no readable name and put in a new motor. My uncle got the mail route and that burned out, rebuilt tug brought up here from the Coos Bay area for the bridgework was the first mail boat he used. He never did put a name on it. He used it for several years hauling mail, fish, cranes, and milk from a creamery in Cushman."

The story of the tug demonstrates the difficulty of getting rid of something by throwing it in the river when tides are involved. On the bridge, dropping wooden scaffolding and forms in the river as a way to get rid of them, inadvertently turned out to be a boon for both towns. Once again, the tides played a role.

A lot of wood was used in building the bridge — 1,500,000 lineal feet to be precise — and almost all of it ended up being tossed in the river. The tides swept some out to sea, but much of it washed up on both sides of the river upstream and down. This was the Depression, a time when nothing was wasted. So folks salvaged this wood. They were out in the river in boats snagging it as well as patrolling the riverbanks for it. They used it, bartered it, or sold it — often by auctioning it off.

The late Goodren Gallo remembered how her folks got their bridge wood. "It took about two years to get enough wood. We were there each time some was auctioned off on our side of the river. Then we had to get the nails all out. We paid for enough to build a house in the Glenada area. That house is still standing and the beams in it are 12 by 12s."

The late Zane Ziemer's family moved to Florence in 1935 and his father got a job at Old Town Garage working for Jack Ponzler, who was in the process of constructing the garage building. "After putting in his eight hours working on vehicles," recalled Ziemer talking about his father, "he put in an hour in the evening, helping install the big timbers in the flooring throughout the building. Later he was up on scaffolding helping place roof trusses. Both the timbers underneath and the trusses above came from the bridge." Some of the bridge wood was big — 30 to 40 feet long and a square foot thick.

Meanwhile upriver, Jensen's playhouse underwent construction. "We had the floor down and were preparing to put up the sides. We had enough wood to make it two stories high. But Dad came home from work about then and gave us some helpful advice that changed our plans. He got us down to one story with lower sides. The dimensions were 10 by 12 feet, and we had a door and one window. I think we eventually built a tin-can heater of some sort. We slept out there a few times and played in it a lot in the summertime. Why, we even had a flower garden around it."

Florence and Glenada were simply ahead of their time; the word "recycling" probably had not even been coined yet. Like the Gallo house, several residences and businesses in the two towns and around the area owed their existence either totally or partially to bridge wood. And several of these buildings still stand today. Ponzler's Old Town Garage is a good example. Today the building is home to Hoberg's Complete Automotive Service. Take a walk slightly downhill behind the building. Then look up underneath the main floor to see the large supporting timbers — bridge wood.

Progress means change

Having a bridge — instead of a ferry — to cross the river changed the behavior of people. Because you didn't have to deal with a ferry, it was much more convenient to cross from one side to the other and you could cross during the night. Driving made it possible to go over and back so much faster, and if you didn't have a car, walking was easy with sidewalks on both sides.

Frank Barrett grew up on the Glenada side in a house overlooking the river and provides an example of what a difference the bridge made to his family during two births. "In 1935, my older sister who lived on the Glenada side was ready to give birth and it was at night. Since the ferry didn't run at night, her husband had to row across the river to get the doctor and bring him across by rowboat to deliver the baby. The next year when I was born, someone ran across the bridge to get Doctor Navarre Dunn and he came over in his car. It was so much easier and faster."

The bridge certainly changed the character of Front Street. On the western end, the street ran right under the bridge — hard to miss it. Front Street was Florence's main street, but that

Bird's Eye View

From the new bridge to where the highway narrows was the new stretch of highway. It bypassed downtown Florence, which was concentrated on the waterfront.

would change. When the ferry was running, the Oregon Coast Highway traffic debarked on Front Street right in downtown. The highway ran right through town. It passed the Kyle Building (Bridgewater restaurant), continued north past Peterson's Automotive (Feast restaurant), curved past the north side of the school (Siuslaw Pioneer Museum), up the hill past the present day Florence Events Center, and past the east end of the present day shopping center at the intersection of the Siuslaw and Coast highways (Quince and Highway 126), and on to connect with the new highway (Highway 101) where Quince joins it.

That was outside the town limits. "The entire town, including the business community, the school and the churches, were all located within a few blocks of the waterfront for the first 50 years of its existence," wrote Bill Calder in 1986 when Florence commemorated the 50th anniversary of the bridge.

The northern approach to the bridge was a straight shot through a less populated section of Florence. Once the bridge opened, this was the new route of the Oregon Coast Highway and it was paved. Until then, Front Street had been the only paved street in town, according to Jensen. A large stretch of dunes reached from the northern end of the bridge to where the Landmark Motel is today. And that separated the new highway from town. In 1938, according to *The Siuslaw Oar*, funds were appropriated to extend Lincoln Street (Laurel Street) to the new highway necessitating a heavy cut through the dunes. All that is left of the stretch of dunes is where the motel is located.

Highway traffic sped straight ahead when coming from the south, bypassing the downtown and most of Florence, unless vehicles knew to turn sharply, immediately after crossing the bridge. "Suddenly, the town's emphasis shifted from the waterfront to the new highway," continued Calder in the same article. "Eager businessmen relocated to the highway in hopes of capturing the business of auto travelers passing through on their way up and down the coast. The commercial strip that started in 1936 reaches for several miles today. Eventually, even the post office and city hall moved from their Front Street locations to the modern highway."

The Oregon Coast Highway became the main street in town, and Front Street became Bay Street on January 5, 1956, when Florence did a major renaming of streets (from president names to tree names) and renumbering of houses and businesses. Not long afterwards, Bay Street fell on hard times that lasted into the late 1970s. Descriptions ranged from "colorful" to "rough." And "respectable" people kept their children away. Then in the '80s the street and whole riverfront area gradually transformed into the tourist-oriented Old Town, which since then has become one of Florence's main tourist attractions.

Safe Passage

A fishing boat heads back to port through a single uplifted span of the Siuslaw River Bridge.

After the bridge was built, Florence was no longer so remote and the town grew — not rapidly but gradually — and there was a major increase in school enrollment.

Calder saw the completion of the bridges as one of the most important events in coastal history. "Their completion marked the beginning of a new era in transportation for the coast. With the highway complete, eager travelers flocked to the coast to see the spectacular scenery. It was the start of a multi-million dollar tourist industry that virtually transformed coastal communities. The construction of the highway, and in particular, the completion of the bridges, virtually ushered in an industry that now rivals logging and fishing as one of the biggest coastal industries," wrote Calder in 1986. During the past 25 years since Calder's article, tourism has continued to grow and has surpassed logging and fishing as the major coastal industry.

CHAPTER 6

~~~

During World War II

THE BRIDGE hadn't aged very much by the time of the United States' involvement in World War II. It was only five years old and still looked new. It's hard to imagine that such a new bridge would be wired with explosives or have mines planted beneath it in order to blow it up in the event of an invasion, but those rumors were rife during the war years. Several old-timers who were youngsters during 1941–45, remembered them and thought they were true. But none of them saw any explosives or mines or had any firsthand experience to confirm them. And neither mines nor wired explosives were confirmed by anyone at the U.S. Coast Guard station in Florence or by historian Christopher Bell at ODOT or the numerous contacts with whom he checked.

Hadlow was one of Bell's contacts and here is his explanation: "As for the 'wired bridge,' I have never heard this story in connection with the Siuslaw River Bridge. The story is usually associated with the Rogue River bridge at Gold Beach during World War II. In fact, on that bridge, the wires were left over from the bridge's construction in the early 1930s, when McCullough had all sorts of monitoring gauges installed on the bridge to measure stress and strain when he was carrying out the Freyssinet technique to pre-stress the arches. The telephone-style wires all went to a small construction shack." This could certainly explain the rumor for the I.L. Patterson Bridge over the Rogue River and by extension could explain the rumors for the Siuslaw River Bridge and others.

"There are a lot of World War II stories (i.e. the Interstate being able to land B-52s, or the like) and such stories — at a very high classified level — could be true (in some specific section of highway), but most of the time it was conjecture on the part of locals," said Bell. "I have not heard anything about mining or wiring the Siuslaw River Bridge with explosives, and we have not found any evidence of this."

There were also rumors involving armaments aimed at the bridge, practice bombing runs nearby, and planes flying under the bridge.

We know for a fact — not rumor — that traffic on the coast was less during the war years because of gasoline rationing, which curtailed local driving and killed tourism. Also, there were many people away from home either fighting overseas or otherwise involved with the war effort. Those who stayed home and had a car did no unnecessary driving.

Included here are comments from interviews with a couple of old-timers who were youngsters living in the area during World War II. Frank Barrett was quite young (5 to 9 years old between 1941–45) and Walt Fossek was seven years older. These are their remembrances.

Siuslaw River Bridge

Everyone is pleased that the bridge wasn't blown up with explosives during World War II — apparently the "wired with explosives" and "mines planted beneath" were only rumors. Notice the different sizes of the supports: the massive bascule pier, the sturdy tied-arch pier, and the graceful bent as seen close up on the Florence side.

Frank Barrett

WE LIVED on the Glenada side overlooking the river not far from where the south approach comes in. I was born the same year as the bridge was completed, so I like to say that I grew up with the bridge. In 2011, we both turn 75. I don't know of anybody who has walked over it as many times as I have.

When I was a kid, I remember the bridge as being so white and smooth — beautiful — and it sparkled in the sun. The road across the bridge was smooth too and had so little traffic during the war years that I used to rollerskate on it. The black asphalt type stuff that was put on the lift span was laid like tile in sections of approximately 4 or 5 feet by 2 feet. And when I skated, I had to be careful not to trip if an edge of one was raised up. Sometimes a section would be missing — had to be real careful then.

My older brother would often go off with his friends and leave me, so I'd go climb a tree and watch for cars crossing the bridge. More than once, I saw Jeeps, army trucks, half-tracks, and army tanks come along. I wondered what it would sound like to be under the bridge and listen to a tank go over. So I climbed down the bank and stood under the bridge. Wow! What a racket those tanks made. They were so heavy, they caused the bridge to move a lot. Actu-

Frank Barrett as a young boy

ally, anything heavy caused the bridge to move a lot. A fair amount of movement was allowed for when the bridge was built, I think. You don't notice the movement on top, but you sure do underneath.

I'd cross the bridge to go over to Florence to play with my friend Bob Rose. One day we heard an army Jeep going up the hill behind where the Dairy Queen is today, so we climbed up the hill and peeked through the bushes. We were surprised to see two large cannons set up: one facing the bridge and one facing downriver toward the mouth. There were also a couple of soldiers. I think one was relieving the other of guard duty. We must have made some noise because one soldier headed in our direction. We were scared and ran down the hill as fast as we could go.

My dad, Howard Barrett Sr., and Ed Tatum [the same guy who fell off the bridge and later became a Florence policeman] were nighttime guards on the bridge during the war years. There was a curfew, I think. They stayed in one of the pier houses on the west side of the bridge and checked any cars that came across. Each night about 11 p.m., my mom and I would walk out on the bridge and take something for my dad to eat. It was exciting, and I would've been scared if I'd been by myself.

Near the end of the war, I was outside playing and saw an airplane go really low over the bridge heading upriver. I watched it; it was an air force plane with two men in leather helmets sitting one behind the other. It circled around and came back and flew under the span on the Florence side. I couldn't believe my eyes. I think it was Bob Kyle because he was in the air force and whenever he could, he would fly upriver and dip his wings for his mom who lived where the Dairy Queen is now.

One Sunday morning when I was about eight, my mom and I were walking across to go to church and a fellow we knew came along in a Model A coupe and asked if we wanted a ride. We said yes and he pulled a U-turn right in the middle of the bridge, and it didn't hold up any traffic. After the war, traffic picked up again.

"I wondered what it would sound like to be under the bridge and listen to a tank go over. So I climbed down the bank and stood under the bridge. Wow! What a racket those tanks made. They were so heavy, they caused the bridge to move a lot. Actually, anything heavy caused the bridge to move a lot."
Frank Barrett

Walt Fossek

~~~~~~

MORE THAN one person told me that this bridge was mined with explosives during World War II. Sure glad they didn't have to use them.

My brother and I were rabid beach-combers, and we were warned not to go on the beach, especially at Siltcoos Outlet. There was an encampment there and guardhouses. Planes from North Bend would come up and take target practice on something called a pyramid, which had a target on all sides. It was located directly west of the southern end of Woahink Lake. We called this area "quicksand flats," and it was in the deflation plain behind the foredune. Because of these planes and their bombing practice, we were convinced that the bridge was indeed mined with explosives.

We stayed off the beach in that area on account of them strafing their targets during target practice runs. They had little bombs about a foot long with a 12-gauge shotgun shell filled with phosphorous, and when they dropped them,

Walt Fossek

Perhaps these reminiscences have helped set the record straight regarding some of the rumors heard during and since the war years.

they would leave a little trail of smoke. We'd find them and collect them when the planes weren't around. I remember one dropped in Woahink Lake, and they called in an explosives expert. We laughed because we had a whole pile we had picked up, and there was no explosive in any of them.

This stretch of coast was patrolled on the beach with horses and men and dogs. Even though we weren't supposed to, we went down to the outlet several times and no one ever challenged us. But we knew it was being patrolled, and the hairs on the backs of our necks would stand on end. We'd stick around a little while before making a hasty retreat.

After the war, we went out to the target area to check it out and got stopped by the quicksand. Throughout the area, though, we picked up bullets from the 50-caliber guns. You could tell the fired ones because they had rifling marks. We also found casings and pressed steel links, and we made ammunition belts out of them. We had a good time. I'll never forget those years.

Arch Rivals

As a rite of passage, many boys during their pre-teen and teen years climbed or walked up and over the bridge arches. Some boys hugged the arches and others used no hands.

CHAPTER 7

～～～

Over the Years

WHEN ASKED to come up with stories having to do with the Siuslaw River Bridge, a few old-timers searched their memories and came up with numerous events and activities that took place during the past 75 years. They are recounted here, giving a feel for life in this river town.

1940s–'60s — Rite of passage

As a rite of passage, many boys during their pre-teen and teen years climbed or walked up and over the bridge arches. The late Don Bowman, who grew up in Florence and later became mayor, confessed that he could never summon the courage to try it. He remembered one kid, though, who climbed up over one arch and then the next again and again, making it look super easy.

Frank Barrett, who grew up almost next door to the bridge, told about his arch-climbing experiences in the late 1940s. "We would climb to the top and stop in the middle and work our way over to the light and sit there, watching the cars down below. Then we would head down the arch. That was the scary part — especially if you came down in the middle because the arches end next to the pier houses not behind them. Going the other way, you could kinda slide down the last part and be stopped by

the pylons. I never did tell my mother."

About 15 years later Lynn Unser, who also grew up in Florence, had similar adventures. "I took a running start with tennis shoes so I could get some momentum. When I got to the top, I'd walk to the center and place a bag over the beacon. That way my buddies could tell I'd been there. Of course, I'd try to go over both arches. The bravest ones were those that came down by one of the pier houses where there was no pylon to help them stop."

Chic Hammon also climbed up and over more than once, not realizing that in later years he would spend more than 20 years working for ODOT and that the bridge would be in his jurisdiction. His cousin, Duke Wells, used to walk over the bridge using no hands, no less.

1964 — Tsunami waves

In 1964 on Good Friday, a 9.2 magnitude earthquake hit Alaska and it generated a series of tsunami waves, which affected the Oregon coast. Because the waves came at night and were spaced an hour or more apart, many people didn't even know about the tsunami until the next day, and not every coastal town sustained damage. The only known Oregon casualties were the

Tug-and-Barge Era

A Sause Brothers tug tows a barge headed upriver for a load of lumber.

children from a family camping at Beverly Beach.

Here's how Barrett remembers it. "My wife woke me about midnight and told me about the Alaskan earthquake and tsunami and how one wave had already hit our area. It was a moonlit night, and I got in my Buick and went across the bridge over to Florence where I could see the Coast Guard boat in the middle of the river out from the cannery (where Mo's is now). I joined about 10 or 12 others who were standing on a dock watching the river. I could see that it was starting to go out really fast and then the dock started dropping. The Coast Guard yelled for everyone to get off the dock cause another wave was coming. I ran and got in my Buick and raced back across the bridge and back home and told my wife to get the kids and head to the top of the hill. But she wouldn't wake the kids.

"I saw a wave of about 15 feet coming upriver and it sounded like a horrible wind but no trees were moving. In front of the wave were a couple boats and logs and root wads — all kinds of stuff. And it hit a float house hard on the Glenada side east of the bridge and knocked it loose. It went sailing upriver with a guy inside who had his head out the window yelling for help, but there was nothing I could do. Les Nordahl, who lived on the Florence side of the river, saw him too. Years later when we were talking about the tsunami, he told me. The wave headed upriver a ways and then kind of spread out. Before long, it starting going out and pushed the float house into piling and then onto sand where the guy was able to get out.

"Les told me also that the first wave knocked out piling and the marina west of the bridge and that's where his brother Trygve's pile driver was tied up. After the first wave, it was loose. So Trygve drove up to Cushman to get his tug and headed downriver back towards Florence when he was hit by the second wave. He told

Les, it was like riding up over the biggest wave imaginable. The next day another wave was expected about noon and the bridge was crowded with expectant people, but nothing happened."

Walt Fossek didn't see the tsunami waves, but he saw the results the next morning. "As the waves came up the river, they peeled along the south side. You could see where they went. Most of the docks and boats were spared because for them it was just a huge swell. But then, I guess it hit the point and rebounded and swirled around and took off the entire sport moorage. It was gone the next morning, except for a dory sitting on top of a piling."

According to Frank Nelson, former bridge engineer with ODOT, "If the Siuslaw River Bridge was hit by a large tsunami, I would not make an assumption that the bridge would be gone. I would expect the main spans to survive."

1960s–'70s — Tug-and-barge era

Fred Jensen grew up along the river between Florence and Mapleton. During the 1960s and '70s when it was the heyday of Mapleton's Davidson Lumber Mill; tug-assisted barges filled with lumber were a common sight on the river. The bridge opened quite regularly in those days to let them through. "Davidson shipped a lot of lumber to Hawaii and the California Bay Area," explained Jensen. "And the Corps of Engineers kept the river dredged all the way from the mouth to the mill because it was so important."

A tug with a barge full of lumber passing under the bridge was a normal sight. But one day, Fossek saw three tugs and their accompanying barges all heading downriver on the same tide. "The bridge tender in those days came up from Reedsport, and his name was Tiny Marsh. Yep, he was a big guy. And he went by the book, which said not to keep the bridge open more than 15 minutes. He let two barges and their tugs through and then closed it to let the Highway 101 traffic pass by. After it thinned, he opened it for the last barge and tug," explained Fossek. Then he shook his head, still bothered by Tiny's decision. "So sad! If he hadn't gone by the book, somewhere between 3 and 4 million board feet of lumber would have passed under the bridge — all in one fell swoop!"

At the height of the lumber shipping, the Sause Brothers were the main shippers of lumber by barge. Taking a barge under the bridge, especially in bad current conditions, takes a lot more skill than most people realize. The fenders that protect the main bridge piers have served their purpose well. Barges have bumped them a number of times, but bent up fender piling are replaceable. "One time," remembered Fossek, "a barge sheared out of control and hit the main pier on the Florence side, I think. Rumor had it that it knocked a hole about three or four feet across near the base, and the hollow inside of that pier started taking in water, and one of the bar owners in Old Town sounded the alarm up and down the street, 'The bridge is sinking! The bridge is sinking!' It generated a lot of fuss, but I think it only knocked off a little bit of concrete — no big hole." In checking with ODOT, no one there could find out anything about a hole knocked in one of the piers.

1960s — Permanent bridge tender wanted

"The bridge was always a handicap to having a big fishing fleet here because of having to open so often and imposing on Highway 101 traffic," said Fossek. "Just a couple three years ago we were sitting on the deck at Traveler's Cove and a fishing boat came by and the bridge opened to let it through. Everything went like clockwork; the whole operation lasted only about 10 minutes. But there were probably about a 100 cars waiting in each direction. One day when the bridge opened, I happened to be pulling onto the highway by the northern end of the bridge. As I drove north, I counted the stopped cars and got to 130 before I had to turn off. It was a normal summer weekday."

As was previously mentioned, this bridge was built with the idea of having a full time bridge tender. "For years the port tried to get one here," said Fossek. "I was fishing my boat *The Otter* out of here, and I raised the mast a height that I could go under the bridge any time. It was the poles that I had to let down. The port decided they wanted me to call on the bridge to open whenever I went out in their efforts to keep someone on full time. I think there actually was someone here for awhile. So every time I went under the bridge, I would leave the poles up so the bridge would have to open. It was kind of embarrassing because they were too big for me to handle at the bar, so I would always have to let them down before I went over it. Seemed like a real inconvenience, and after awhile, I quit doing it. They never did get enough traffic to have a permanent bridge tender."

1970s — Spectacular stunts . . . almost

No one remembered any suicides from the bridge, but Duke Wells, the no-hands arch walker, told about jumping into the river from the bridge more than once when he was a teenager. And some years ago on his 50th birthday, he celebrated by diving into the river from the cement railing by the arch on the Florence side — in December, no less. Several friends were witnesses.

But Barrett witnessed the biggest stunt. "One year on the Fourth of July, a guy was going to dive off the bridge from the top of the arch on the Glenada side," he explained. "He was supposed to jump at noon and a crowd had gathered along the waterfront and on the bridge. He didn't show and, finally, the police searched

50-Year Rededication

Onlookers applaud as Bill Karnowsky and Gail Darling Fowler (1936 Queen Rhododendra) begin drive across the bridge in May 1986.

for him and found him in a Bay Street tavern. They drug him out and brought him to the bridge. He climbed up to the top and just stood there and stood there. The crowd became restive. All of a sudden he dove, and we were on the bridge right under him. His hands were spread apart — not together. His head hit hard and he disappeared under the water. A boat came over to help, and he surfaced and went under again. The next time he surfaced, they drug him aboard. I don't think he really wanted to jump."

Fossek continues the story. "The fellow who jumped was a professional dare devil and was in the habit of going to various bars and taking bets. And he bet that he could jump off the bridge. To up the ante, he decided to jump from the top of one of the arches. At the time he wanted to jump, he had to wait because a boat unexpectedly passed under. Somehow, it must have affected his timing. Instead of making a graceful dive, he barely cleared the railing and ended up doing the mother of all belly flops. The splash was almost as high as the deck of the bridge. It didn't kill him, but it bruised him up pretty bad. He collected his winnings, which he more than earned.

"In Coos Bay, he tried a more spectacular stunt, at least that's how he presented it. Since he had jumped off the bridge in Florence, he didn't need to jump off the bridge over Coos Bay. He decided to jump from a plane over the bay with no parachute and bet big money. He waited till afternoon when the wind was blowing about 40 miles per hour and chartered a light plane. It flew low over the water, about 6 to 8 feet off the waves. He was moving along against a 40 mile-per-hour wind, so the plane is only moving 10 or 15 miles per hour over water — hardly even water-skiing speed. So the guy jumps into the water and his boat was waiting to pick him up. He collected his winnings, which was a lot easier money than jumping off the Siuslaw River Bridge."

1986 — 50th Anniversary and rededication

Senator Mark Hatfield attended and spoke along with Florence Mayor Wilbur Ternyik at the 50th anniversary celebration of the bridge. But the story that most old-timers remembered was that of long-time resident Bill Karnowsky who had a garage on Bay Street practically under the bridge.

Karrol Martin wrote in the *Siuslaw News* April 1993 Centennial issue about the first car to cross the new bridge in 1936. "The duel was between a Rickenbacker coupe and a Whippet sedan, the latter driven by Bill Karnowsky. 'I started out first,' Bill recollected, stroking his chin, 'but I stopped to clear away some debris. The engine stalled, and as I tried to get 'er started, the Rickenbacker slipped right on by me.'"

Bill had worked as a construction laborer on the bridge during 1935–36, and looked forward to being the first car to cross the bridge when it opened. After waiting 50 years, he got a second chance. He was at the 50th anniversary and rededication of the bridge in May 1986. He proudly drove a Model A Ford and sitting next to him was Gail Darling Fowler, who as Queen Rhododendra christened the bridge 50 years earlier.

1990s — Accolades

"The Siuslaw River Bridge is a good bridge to walk to appreciate McCullough's attention to detail," wrote Elliot Diamond in *The Sunday Oregonian* in December 1994. "Its finely sculptured Art Deco obelisks, Gothic arch railings, and approach pylons transform the . . . concrete structure into a monument of impressive yet unpretentious beauty."

In October 1999, national attention was focused on the bridge because of the *USA Today* article, "10 Great Places to Cross the Water." The Siuslaw River Bridge was the only bridge selected in the entire state considered worthy of a detour. "Built during the great public works era of the Depression," wrote Gene Sloan, "this is the most stunning of the 'extraordinary bridges, no two alike' along the Oregon Coast."

2005 — National Register Listing

The Siuslaw River Bridge, along with 10 other McCullough coastal bridges, was nominated by ODOT and approved by the governor-appointed State Advisory Committee on Historic Preservation to be listed on the National Register of Historic Places. The bridges were grouped in a multiple property submission, recognizing the work of Oregon bridge engineer Conde B. McCullough, and listed in November 2005.

This was a great honor for the Siuslaw River Bridge and the other coastal bridges designed by McCullough.

"The Siuslaw River Bridge is a good bridge to walk to appreciate McCullough's attention to detail. Its finely sculptured Art Deco obelisks, Gothic arch railings, and approach pylons transform the . . . concrete structure into a monument of impressive yet unpretentious beauty."
Elliot Diamond
The Sunday Oregonian
December 1994

McCullough Coastal Bridges on the National Register

~~~~~~~

Listed North to South

• WILSON RIVER BRIDGE (1931) one 120-foot reinforced-concrete through tied arch, total length 180 feet, Tillamook vicinity, Tillamook County.

• DEPOE BAY BRIDGE (1927/1940) two 150-foot reinforced-concrete deck arches (side by side), total length 312 feet, Depoe Bay, Lincoln County. (Except for being slightly wider, an identical bridge was built alongside the original 13 years later, making four lanes to match up with the highway on either end.)

• ROCKY CREEK BRIDGE (also called the Ben Jones Bridge) (1927) one 160-foot reinforced-concrete deck arch, total length 360 feet, Otter Crest vicinity, Lincoln County.

• YAQUINA BAY BRIDGE (1936) one 600-foot steel through arch, two 350-foot steel deck arches, five reinforced-concrete deck arches, total length 3,223 feet, Newport, Lincoln County.

• TEN MILE CREEK BRIDGE (1931) one 120-foot reinforced-concrete through tied arch, total length 180 feet, Yachats vicinity, Lane County.

• BIG CREEK BRIDGE (1931) one 120-foot reinforced-concrete through tied arch, total length 235 feet, Heceta Head vicinity, Lane County.

• CAPE CREEK BRIDGE (1932) one 220-foot reinforced-concrete deck arch, total length 619 feet, Heccta Hcad vicinity, Lanc County.

• SIUSLAW RIVER BRIDGE (1936) one 140-foot double-leaf bascule steel draw span, two 154-foot reinforced-concrete through tied arches, total length 1,568 feet, Florence, Lane County.

• UMPQUA RIVER BRIDGE (1936) one 430-foot steel through truss tied arch swing span, four 154-foot reinforced-concrete through tied arches, total length 2,206 feet, Reedsport, Douglas County.

• McCULLOUGH MEMORIAL BRIDGE (1936) one 793-foot and two 457½-foot steel cantilever truss spans, 13 reinforced-concrete deck arches, total length 5,305 feet, North Bend, Coos County.

• I.L. PATTERSON BRIDGE (1932) seven 230-foot reinforced-concrete deck arches, total length 1,898 feet, Gold Beach, Curry County.

The National Register of Historic Places was created under the authority of the National Historic Preservation Act of 1966 as a listing of districts, sites, archaeological sites, buildings, structures, and objects of national, state, and local significance.

PART III
IMPROVEMENTS & THE FUTURE

‿‿‿

CHAPTER 8
Renovations

FOR THE FIRST FOUR DECADES after it was built, the Siuslaw River Bridge required only routine maintenance — cleaning, painting, and minor repairs. In 1969, 120 new 75-foot-long creosoted piling were driven in 25 feet deep to replace old deteriorating piling that had been protecting the bridge's main piers. It wasn't until the 1970s and then again 30 years later that major repairs and/or changes were made to the bridge itself, and both times they involved only the road deck on the lift spans.

In a March 2001 article, "Turning 65," in the *Siuslaw News*, reporter John Fiedler quoted ODOT bridge inspector Jeff Swanstrom, "The bridge at 65 is aging gracefully. We think the dunes out there are protecting it from the harsh elements." The dunes do block somewhat the winter storm winds out of the southwest, and the bridge isn't as close to the ocean and its salt spray as some of the other reinforced-concrete bridges. Maybe that's why it took 73 years before major repairs to the bridge as a whole were required.

Replacing bascule road deck

The original bascule deck of Port Orford cedar surfaced with asphalt connecting tiles (noted as asphalt planks in the original specs) was replaced in 1977, when constant patching made it no longer workable. The road deck was replaced with a steel grid, which, lighter in weight, made it easier for the bascule mechanism to lift. But it was also noisy. Folks in Old Town anywhere near the bridge could hear quite a rumble each time a vehicle drove over the grid.

The noise became an issue over the years as traffic increased and Florence's Old Town became a popular tourist destination. Besides the noise, the metal grid was becoming fatigued and ODOT bridge crews were continually repairing cracked welds. When larger sections began to crack, it became a safety concern. In spring 2005, the lift span's road deck was replaced and the sidewalks redone. The sidewalks were replaced by composite decking. The metal grid was replaced with a fiberglass-reinforced polymer decking with a half-inch polymer concrete wearing surface sealed with urethane epoxy. It not only made the bridge less noisy, but it strengthened the structure. At the same time down below, the wood planking on the pointed dolphin fenders protecting the east and west sides of the main piers were replaced with black fiberglass-reinforced plastic timbers.

"Paving was really a godsend to those who lived and worked in Old Town near the bridge," said old-timer Fred Jensen.

Before starting the 2005 project, ODOT worked with the community and, in particular, the Merchants of Old Town to make the noise and inconvenience of the roadwork as bearable as possible. After completion, the nearby businesses were so pleased they put up a banner publicly thanking ODOT and had plaques made. "I called ODOT and the person I talked to couldn't believe that we wanted to make a big deal of thanking them," said Florence resident Loretta Hoagland then co-owner of the River House, a motel located close to the bridge. "He called back a while later and asked if his boss could come, and then called again to see if his boss's boss could come. Nobody wanted to be left out. They were used to getting flak, but not this appreciation stuff. On June 5, 2005, the plaques were presented and the story and photo were in the local paper."

Making its needs known in 2009

The bridge was slated for its first major overhaul and facelift to begin June 2009. But just a few months earlier, the bridge let everyone know that after 73 years, it was about time. On Friday February 27, the bridge got stuck with one lift span in the open position. According to Michael Russell writing in *The Oregonian*, "After letting a fishing boat go under, a bridge operator was closing the Siuslaw River Bridge about 4:40 p.m. when an electrical

fire left the southern section in the 'up' position. The northern section lowered successfully. Traffic was backed up for miles in both directions." More than one bridge tender would be needed to handle this problem.

"A crew drove from Charleston, over an hour's drive to the south," wrote Russell, "and they used a large wrench to manually release the braking system and manually lower the bridge by about 7:15 p.m."

Florence Mayor Phil Brubaker found humor in the situation. "I told people with a straight face that this was a new tourism development program," he said with a grin. "We're going to get the bridge stuck every Friday afternoon right at happy hour and then everyone has to go down to Bay Street and wait."

Major improvements begin

Renovations began the first week of June 2009. They were part of a $5.3-million project to modernize the historic bridge with Hamilton Construction of Springfield, Oregon, as contractor and ODOT inspectors checking every step along the way. The project planned to replace the aging manual/electrical lift system with a new, state-of-the-art computer and video system, restore the four pier houses and the two main piers, replace electrical components, strengthen parts of the bridge, paint the lift spans, and pressure wash the concrete sections.

"We were just so fortunate to have the stimulus package and the bridge repair fund that made it possible to work on the bridge," said Mayor Brubaker. President Obama's 2009 stimulus package was a two-year, nationwide effort to jump-start jobs that included rebuilding crumbling roads and bridges.

The bridgework was to be completed by September 2010, but more work was required than had been initially planned. "More sections of bad concrete were chipped out and replaced than anticipated and more rebar repair was needed. On the steel, replaced rivets numbered 2,026 instead of the estimated 500. And bolts instead of rivets were used to replace them," explained ODOT Inspector Nate Neal. "We made sure the smooth side of the bolts showed, so that it still had the rivet look."

Neal also described other improvements decided upon after work had begun. These included placing backlit STOP signs in the recesses in the pylons at the entrance to the tied arches when the red light comes on and replacing the rotted wood bumpers on the navigation channel sides of the main piers with fiberglass-reinforced plastic. It's the same material used on the pointed fenders protecting the pier's east and west sides.

Among planned improvements that might be noticed are new gates, smaller LED lighted aviation beacons, soft lighting in the entry pylons at both ends of the bridge, and low-pressure sodium lights on the piers (provided by the city). Not so noticeable, explained Neal, are the freshwater line

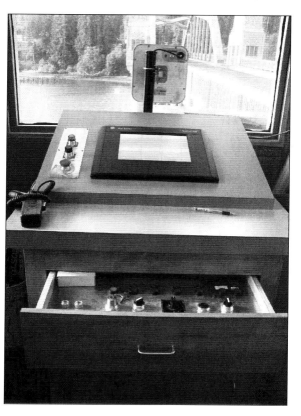

Main Control Room

New computerized control panel with back-up system in the drawer in the northeast pier house on the Siuslaw River Bridge.

added for bridge maintenance and electrical power that now comes from both sides of the river.

Nothing was simple. "The green bascule span required sandblasting before painting the zinc rich primer followed by an intermediate coat and then a top coat of urethane," Neal went on. "And before painting, steel that was badly corroded had to be replaced. Again, more had to be replaced than was planned for."

A barge located under the bridge held compressors and paint equipment during the project.

The pier houses received a major facelift inside and out. New stainless steel doors and bulletproof glass in windows were added to protect the new equipment inside. "This new equipment, sensitive to moisture and temperature, required a warm, dry environment, which in turn required some major engineering," Neal explained. "So the roofs were treated with concrete sealer, an impervious ceiling was installed inside with a drain system that routes moisture through a pipe to the outside. And a circulating air system keeps the air moving above a drop ceiling that hides the mechanics of the new systems."

Every electrical component was replaced. "We think it was all original equipment. If it wasn't, it certainly looked like it," said Neal. Instead of a wall filled with switches and fuse boxes, everything is in its own self-contained unit and these control units fill the northwest and southwest pier houses, which are now called the Motor Control Centers. Each unit stands about as high as a person and is labeled — navigation lights, bascule motor, communication, just to name a few. Each pier house Center controls one side of the bridge, and the two sets of control units are identical. From these two pier houses you cannot access the lower areas down inside the main piers.

Within the Pier

A worker stands on the new staircase within the bascule pier to repair a light fixture.

The other two pier houses on the east side are the Control Rooms, and they have each been upgraded with computerized table-top panels for raising the lift spans. The northeast Control Room is the primary one and will normally be used to operate the bridge and now has new video cameras to monitor traffic. The southeast room is considered back up. These are both computer-controlled, and each can operate both the Glenada side and the Florence side of the bridge. "In case of computer failure, there is also a non-computer controlled back-up system in the Control Rooms," Neal explained. "Each operates only its side of the bridge; so there would need to be two operators working in tandem to open and close both sides of the bridge."

Stairs lead from each of the Control Rooms to their respective piers below. The stairs in the main one — the northeast Control Room — were replaced with a staircase to make access easier. The other one still has a ladder-like stairway.

Housed within each main pier is the machinery that opens the bridge as well as the huge counterweight that makes it all work. In both piers, work was done to seal out moisture as well as general repair and replacement work.

The trunnion, the pivot point in each pier, is located at the base of the stairs. Attached to the trunnion is the machine room where motors turn the reduction gears that move the counterweight that makes the bascule span lift. Hinged access doors that make it easier to get to all parts of the gears for maintenance were part of the bridge renovation.

Other bridge improvements included strengthening the tied arch spans by adding fiber reinforced polymer to the bottom of the deck and floor beams, and pressure washing the tied arches and the four piers that support them.

Not without a few problems

The road deck, not counting the bascule span portion, was given an overlay that "adds years of life to the concrete," said Neal.

"The overlay consisted of applying a two-part epoxy followed by 1/4-inch aggregate blown on," explained Ron Beatty, whose crew did the actual work, "and then the whole process was repeated for a second layer." It was easy to see how much smoother it made the road surface. This process took longer than scheduled, however, due to the weather.

On the day the overlay was scheduled, the morning fog was extra drippy and hung around longer than usual. Since this process is humidity sensitive, the crew waited until it was dry enough. By then the mid-day August traffic was terrific. Consequently, there were hours-long delays, causing unhappy tourists and townspeople, which made the regional news. Because it was going to take another day, there were delays the next day too. The other

New Road Overlay

Bridge improvements included a new overlay on the deck. The right hand lane in this photo shows the new epoxy/aggregate surface.

lane on the bridge, however, was postponed until mid-September when fewer tourists would be on the road. At that time, according to Beatty, part of the work was completed before rain caused another postponement. It was eventually completed in October.

Completing the overlay wasn't the only problem encountered during the renovation work. About a week after the August traffic delay, the bridge was attempting to open for a sailboat, and one of two actuator motors that operates the span locks malfunctioned. The bridge remained partially open for an hour until it was temporarily repaired. Later a permanent fix was worked out.

Although the project encountered more work and took longer than anticipated and had a few problems, it accomplished its major goal of helping prepare the bridge for the future. "The project will extend the service life of the bridge for many years," said ODOT project manager Chuck Lemos.

Early benefits to community

The bridgework had perfect timing as far as those involved in the summer 2010 dredging project were concerned. The boat turning basin fronting Old Town just north of the bridge and the navigation channel in the middle of the river were dredged. For the boat basin it was the first significant cleaning since 1974. Because the dredging spoils were dumped offshore in an approved dump site, that meant the bridge had to open and close three or four times a day to accommodate a tall tug pushing a large scow filled with the dredge material. "Since the computerized systems were not completely ready," explained Neal, "the back-up systems were used with two people, one in each Control Room, communicating by radio as they operated the new non-computerized control panels." Opening and closing this often was more activity than the bridge had seen in a long time, so it was a good test of the new back-up system. Prior to the dredging project, fewer than 10 openings a month would've been the norm. The antiquated system the bridge had been operating with for 73 years might not have been up to the task.

When the old control panel from the northeast pier house was removed, it was loaned to the Siuslaw Pioneer Museum in Florence along with the wall of switches, aviation beacons, and other lights. "Items from the bridge that will be housed at the museum had to pass through the city on the way," explained Mayor Brubaker. "They are state property and as such, have an exacting process for disposal. They are to be put up for auction. Well, we didn't want people buying these historic items and neither did ODOT. So they placed them on permanent loan to the city as long as they are on display." The folks at the museum were so thrilled to receive the historic items, that they added a room for the sole purpose of displaying them. Now everyone can see what it was like to have been a bridge tender on the Siuslaw River Bridge.

Preserving the Old

The old electrical panel replaced during the upgrade is now on display at the Siuslaw Pioneer Museum.

CHAPTER 9

~~~~~

Looking Ahead

Those who look ahead wonder what will happen to the Siuslaw River Bridge in 20 to 30 years when a two-lane bridge may not be up to the traffic loads. That concern, however, will be moot if the bridge is not safe enough for vehicles to cross over. And that is exactly what will happen if the cathodic protection process is not applied in the next few years. Even with the past two years of renovations, the bridge will crumble away over the next few decades without impressed current zinc cathodic protection.

The good news is that this process has already been applied to nine of the Oregon coast's reinforced-concrete bridges. The Mc-Cullough Bridge, currently undergoing the process, is the tenth and the Siuslaw River Bridge will be next, followed by the Umpqua River Bridge. By then, it will be time to start recoating. Because there should be little or no corrosion, recoating the zinc will be the primary component of the work, and the job will go much faster.

So what is this process, this panacea, that can determine the fate of the reinforced concrete bridges of the Oregon coast?

Applying cathodic protection

Back in the 1970s, ODOT maintenance crews concluded that coastal bridges were corroding faster than they could be repaired. As the rebar within the concrete corroded, it swelled, cracking the concrete around it — thus accelerating the process. And in the 1980s, when it was determined that the Alsea Bay Bridge was too far gone to save and had to be replaced, it came as a wake-up call that something major had to be done to save the other bridges. So an engineering team, under the leadership of ODOT bridge engineer Frank Nelson, was charged with figuring out how to restore the bridges to their original condition and preserve them from further deterioration.

The process that they came up with to work with Oregon bridges was called zinc cathodic protection, an electrical process used for years on ships and pipelines, based on the long-accepted anode–cathode process. When applied to reinforced concrete bridges, the existing steel rebar acts as the negative and the zinc coating as the positive, which means that the zinc draws the corrosion away from the rebar and is sacrificed over time. This also means that every 20 or 30 years, the zinc needs to be replaced.

The team, under the leadership of Walt Eager, developed a concrete repair system and adapted the zinc coating process for the coast bridges. These were first used on small bridges before trying on larger ones. In 1991, the Cape Creek Bridge became

the world's first fully electrified, zinc-coated bridge.

In each situation before any work even begins, a containment enclosure must be erected that is designed to withstand winds of 90 miles per hour and is equipped with a heating, dehumidifying, and negative air system capable of maintaining a 70-degree Fahrenheit temperature. The enclosure serves two important purposes — to contain and collect all debris, including chipped concrete, spent abrasives, and zinc waste, to prevent contamination of the environment and water, and to provide a controlled and safe environment for the zinc spray operation and workers. After the enclosure is built, the concrete is sandblasted in order to clean it thoroughly.

Only then can the surveys for problems and repair work begin. Each survey is marked with color-coded chalk marks. The first survey, done by sounding with a hammer, locates damaged concrete and boundaries are marked. The second survey uses metal detectors and visual inspection to locate and mark surface metals or metals within a half inch of the surface. The third survey uses a meter to locate and mark shallow rebar. The bad concrete is chipped out and replaced with a 16-step process. It takes far fewer steps to chip or drill out unwanted pieces of metal and to patch with concrete. And the process for chipping away around the rebar involves the 16 steps as well as testing for electrical continuity and marking those that don't conduct. And, of course, the concrete patches over the rebar have to be made thicker.

Removing Damaged Concrete

A worker on the McCullough Bridge chips away at damaged concrete.

Crucial to extending the life of the bridge is making sure every piece of rebar within the concrete touches another, so the electrical current flows continuously through every inch of connected steel. Those metallic objects within a half inch of the surface must be removed to prevent the zinc coating from short-circuiting with the rebar. Any damaged or deteriorated rebar must be replaced. Where electrical conductivity is still a problem, wiring may have to be added between segments of rebar.

Because the surveys and concrete preparation aspect of the cathodic protection process were actually taking place on the southern end of the McCullough Bridge over Coos Bay during fall 2010, the author was able to see it firsthand. The action took place 90 feet above the water but still under the road deck within the containment enclosure. It took an elevator to get there. Great Western Corporation was the subcontractor in charge of the concrete repair and zinc application with approximately 15 workers on the job. For those working immediately under

Setting Forms

A worker sets forms in preparation for concrete repair.

the road deck, walking on the scaffold flooring was easy, as long as you ducked under the concrete arches. The hard hat came in handy more than once. For those working on the columns below, it was not so easy; they had to work while being suspended by harnesses.

Seeing the work in progress made it easier to understand. Orange chalk marks outlined damaged concrete, red marked where metallic objects needed to be removed, and blue marked rebar that did not conduct electricity. Workers were listening intently while tapping with hammers, chipping out concrete, building forms for the concrete patches, drilling anchor holes to hold the concrete forms, and the ODOT inspector moved from location to location checking on each step. The process is so time consuming, that it will take four years to complete the southern end of the McCullough Bridge. This bridge happens to be the largest cathodic protection project ever attempted in Oregon. The concrete areas are divided into 37 zones to regulate the impressed current consistently and effectively. Completion is expected in 2011. Then it's on to the northern end, which should take about five years.

When the southern end is completed, ODOT engineers will control the low-voltage electrification of the bridge from Salem, tracking the rate of corrosion with monitors inside and outside the bridge and adjusting the current as needed. The inside monitors are installed in the concrete alongside rebar in "hot spots," areas of greatest corrosive activity, which have been determined after performing an in-depth corrosion potential survey on the entire southern end of the bridge. Each zone will monitor two hot spots.

When everything is ready for the zinc coating, the concrete needs to be sandblasted again to rid it of dust, chalk marks, and any other contaminants.

A worker, wearing what looks like a spacesuit with its own fresh air source, applies the 99.9 percent zinc. That worker holds a device that acts like an arc welder where the zinc comes in the form of two 1/8-inch thick wires that melt when hit by a 1200-degree jolt of electricity just as a blast of air blows it onto the concrete surface. There it reforms as a solid layer protecting the coated concrete.

The electrical wiring is added as the last step and is connected to a datalogger and phone line source that is then connected to ODOT engineers in Salem.

It's a complicated process that takes years and then it has to be re-zinced periodically. But it works! By short-circuiting the natural corrosion process, zinc cathodic protection adds decades of useful life to the bridges of the Oregon coast.

Enduring town symbol

Meanwhile, the Siuslaw River Bridge lives the good life in Florence. After its almost two years of renovation, it looks better than it's looked since it was built. Even though the bridge officially belongs to ODOT,

Cathodic Protection

This section of the bridge has been restored and coated with zinc.

the town claims it as its own. Everywhere from the Chamber of Commerce logo to every other page of the Pacific Publishing phone book are images of the bridge. Many town businesses have the bridge in either their logo or their advertising. It's an essential part of the town.

"The Siuslaw River Bridge is our symbol, our icon along with the rhododendron blossom. So the logo you see with the chamber of commerce incorporates both," says Florence Mayor Phil Brubaker. Then he added, "The future of the bridge is based on looking at and respecting the past and the history that surrounds it."

When asked if the bridge would be replaced in the future to build a larger four-lane structure, he responded, "I personally think the answer is never!"

Then he explained how the town's growth spurt of the 1980s and '90s has slowed down in recent years, and he doesn't see it returning to its previous pace. "Looking at our 2020 plan and beyond, our population forecast for 2030 and 2040 is only about double what it is now. Within the city limits, we are just under 10,000, and the outside city limits in the greater Florence area from county line to county line, Sea Lion Caves to Carter Lake, is 17,000. That's not going to double. The city component might as we infill with housing on some of the lots. But I would be very surprised if Florence's population in the next 20 years is more than 15,000."

Then he added, "We're surrounded by national forestlands and by geographic imperatives — one of which is the Pacific Ocean."

The mayor feels that Highway 101 is a bigger question than how many Florence folks use the bridge going back and forth. Because the whole coast is limited by the same geographical constraints and the ocean offshore is currently undergoing major debates on how to manage it, Brubaker thinks the whole coast is going to be an intensively managed resource for the foreseeable future. "That will bring with it not only a healthy respect for the past but put some real limits on how much through traffic there will be. We'll always have our summer influx of tourists; that's one of our real benefits."

Bottom line, "So we'll have that coastal highway, but our little stretch of four-lane that goes a few miles within city limits is going to be it. I don't ever see that extending southward to where we'll need a four-lane bridge."

According to an article in the *Siuslaw News* by Eric Fetters in 1996, when traffic reaches 29,500 trips across the bridge a day, a new bridge will be needed. ODOT's latest numbers from 2008 were 10,700 trips a day.

Highlighting history and ecology

People often ask the mayor about the old ferry landing that was located where the gazebo and a small park are today. "There is an overlook area there now with a platform, but it doesn't include the ramp or being able to walk out on the river because we haven't any dock there. So that observation deck is our historical nod to

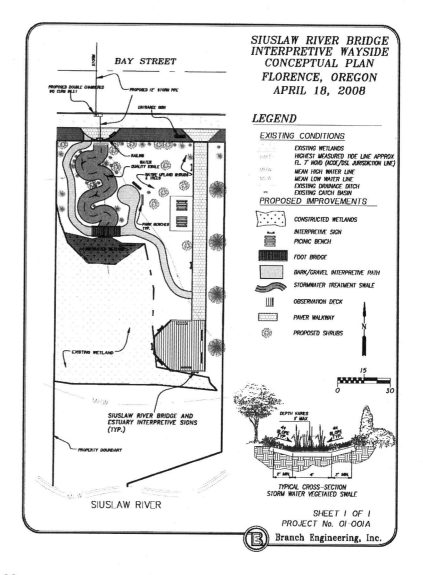

the days of the ferry before the bridge was there."

When asked what has happened to the plan for a bridge interpretive center, the mayor explained that it has changed. "The original plan called for it to be under the bridge, but that changed when we looked at it in terms of our downtown urban renewal plan. We want to preserve the open space between the Siuslaw River Coffee Roasters & Coffee Shop and the Waterfront Depot restaurant, which is a very popular area for viewing the bridge. We just recently [November 2010] completed the negotiations to acquire that property for our interpretive area."

According to Jacque Betz, Florence's assistant city manager, the planned Siuslaw River Bridge Interpretive Wayside will have a dual role. "The wayside will include interpretive signing to introduce visitors to the history of the bridge and surrounding area as well as highlight the ecological value of the estuary." A walkway will lead to an observation deck at the edge of the river, and a fir-bark path will curve around a storm-water treatment swale that will be filled with vegetation, cross a footbridge, pass wetlands, and connect with the walkway to the observation deck. Both the walkway and deck will be constructed of long-lasting plastic composite decking. That deck — so close to the river — should have one of the best views of the bridge in Old Town.

"In addition to the main overlook area," continued Betz, "a small parking area will also be created under the bridge to serve the wayside and provide additional parking for those visiting Old

The Florence Area Chamber of Commerce logo featuring the Siuslaw River Bridge and native rhododendrons.

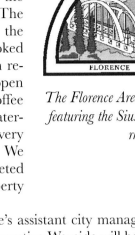

Town." Besides parking, this location will have two overlooks with benches for viewing the bridge. This view from below the bridge shows the cathedral-like quality of the Gothic arches that are such a favorite of local photographers.

With cathodic protection to preserve the reinforced concrete and limited growth making the necessity for a four-lane bridge unlikely, maybe, just maybe, the Siuslaw River Bridge has a realistic chance of being around to celebrate its second 75 years. A lot of folks certainly hope so. And soon there will be a wayside where everyone can stop to admire this very special McCullough bridge.

Without McCullough and the Coast Bridges Project, the Siuslaw River Bridge as well as the four others — Yaquina Bay, Alsea Bay, Umpqua River, and Coos Bay (McCullough Memorial) bridges — would not have been built as the cutting edge masterpieces that they were. In the case of the new Alsea Bay Bridge, it, too, was considered cutting edge because of the excessive protections against corrosion and extremely deep supports and a masterpiece in design because of trying to match the aesthetic appeal of McCullough's original. In 2011 the four original bridges celebrate their 75th anniversary and the new one its 20th. If McCullough could be here, he would see that his bridges are still considered masterpieces. And, no doubt, he would be pleased to see that his "jeweled clasps," as he referred to them, continue to be functional as well as beautiful and have become beloved coastal icons.

Fireworks over the Bridge

The sky over the Siuslaw River is lit by the rockets' red glare as Fourth of July revelers watch the fireworks show.

Wild Roses

Wild roses that grow in a soon-to-be Siuslaw River Bridge Interpretive Wayside frame the newly-renovated bridge.

Appendix 1 • Architectural Drawings

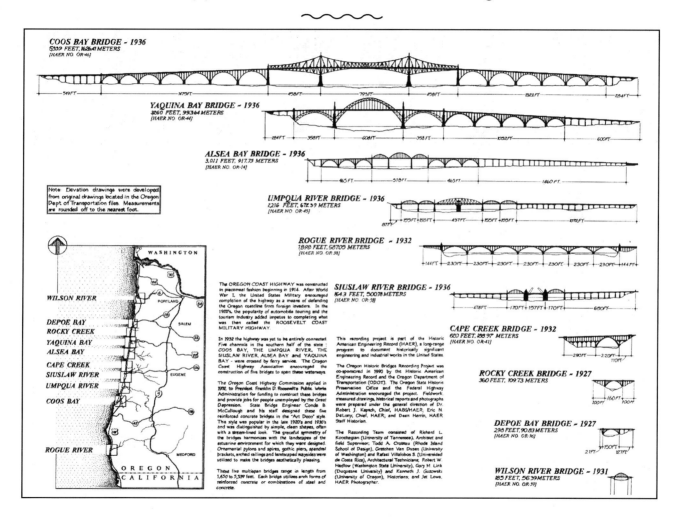

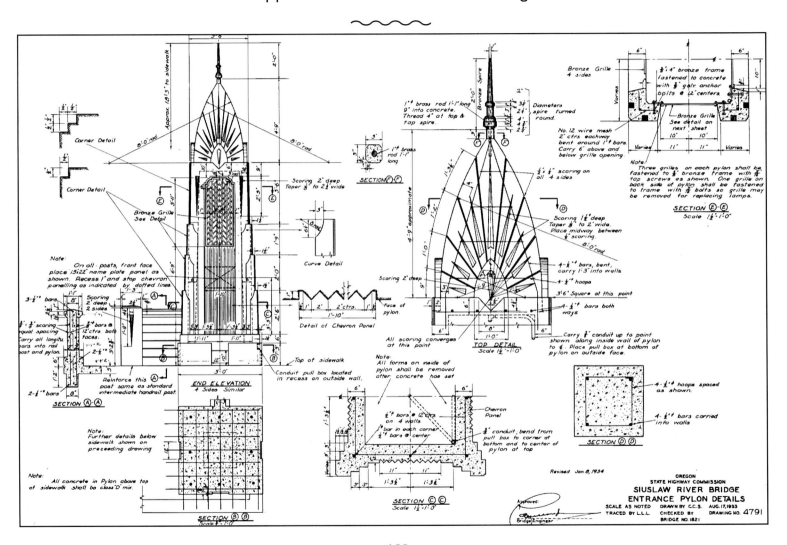

Appendix 1 • Architectural Drawings

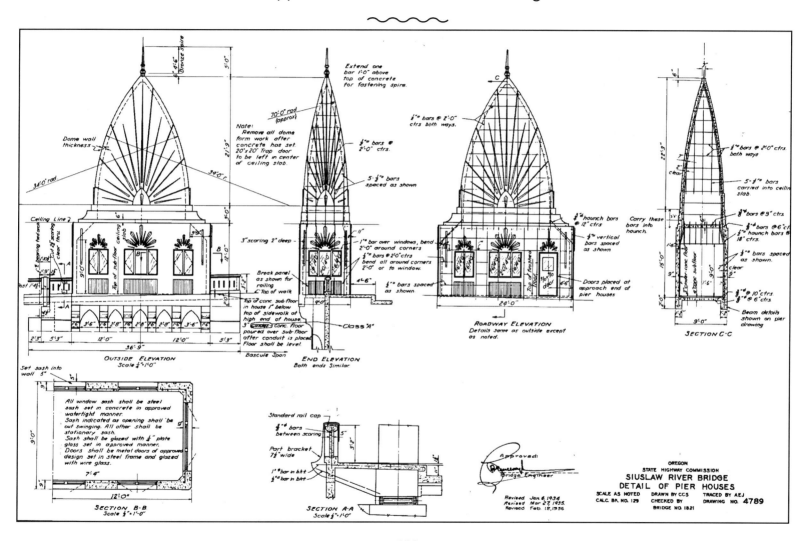

Appendix 1 • Architectural Drawings

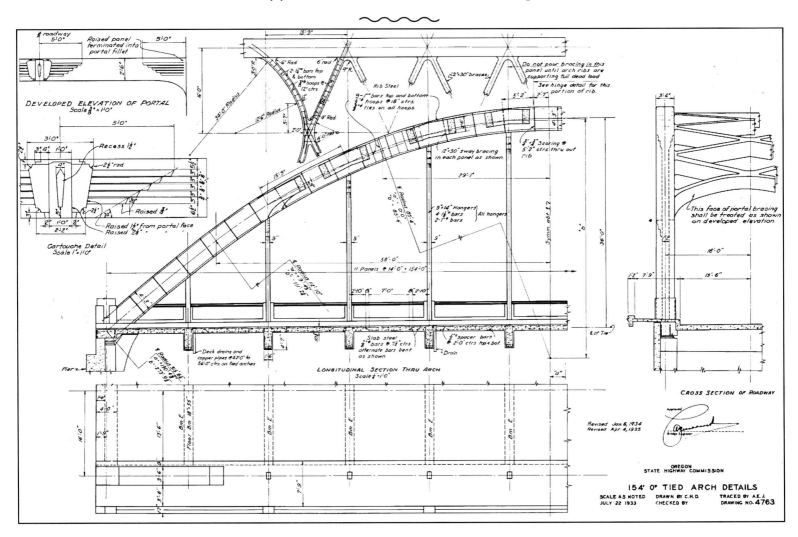

Appendix 1 • Architectural Drawings

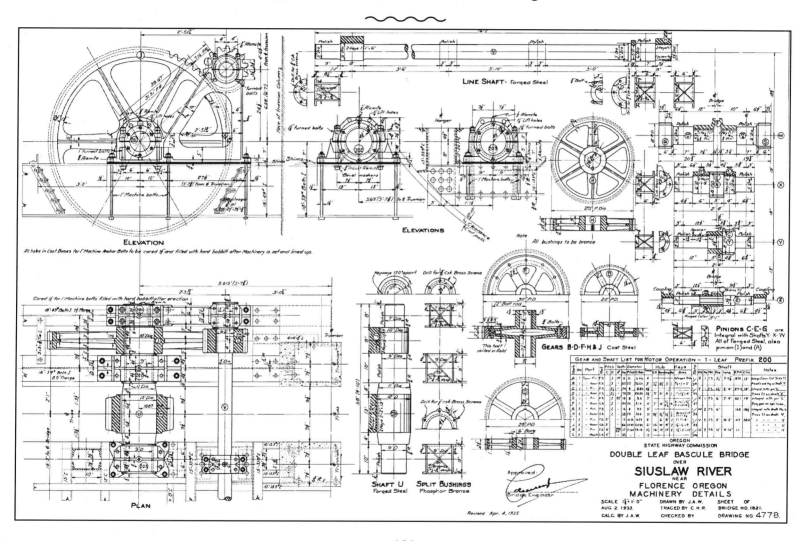

Dusk

The Siuslaw River paints a mirror image of its bridge as the sun goes down over the Pacific Ocean.

Appendix 2 • Books of Similar Interest

• *Bridges: A History of the World's Most Famous and Important Spans*, by Judith Dupre and introductory interview with Frank O. Gehry, Black Dog & Leventhal Publishers, NY, 1997

• *Bridges of the Oregon Coast*, by Ray Bottenberg, Arcadia Publishers, Images of America Series, Charleston, SC, 2006

• *Elegant Arches, Soaring Spans, C.B. McCullough, Oregon's Master Bridge Builder*, by Robert W. Hadlow, Oregon State University Press, Corvallis, OR, 2001

• *Lifting Oregon Out of the Mud, Building the Oregon Coast Highway*, by Joe R. Blakely, Bear Creek Press, Wallowa, OR, 2006

Sway Braces

These sway braces connect the two sides of a tied arch.

Ghosts

Old piling rise from the bottom of the bay as reminders of Florence's past when canneries and sawmills lined the riverbank.

Glossary

This glossary is excerpted from Bridges of the Oregon Coast. *The book and glossary were written by Ray Bottenberg, who graciously granted permission to use herein. Italicized segments were added by the author and are not from Bottenberg's book.*

BALUSTRADE — *A stone or concrete railing, usually decorative, with individual supports called balusters.*

BASCULE-TYPE DRAWBRIDGE — A movable bridge type having one (single leaf) or two (double leaf) spans hinged at a pier, to open upward away from the navigation channel (see Siuslaw River Bridge).

BATTER PILING — A piling driven at a slight angle, used where resistance to horizontal loading is needed.

BENT — A vertical structure, supporting the spans of a bridge, typically on land.

BOWSTRING ARCH — *Another name for a tied arch. The arch is like an archer's bow with the string or tie connecting one end to the other. In this way, the arch is held in compression and the tie in tension. These arches are used where it is not feasible or not desired to support the arch horizontally at ground level.*

BPR — *Bureau of Public Roads*

CANTILEVER — A type of truss in which the main span is supported by two piers at each end (see Coos Bay Bridge).

CARTOUCHE — A scroll-like figure.

COFFERDAM — Temporary structure, typically made by driving sheet piling around an in-water work area, such as in bridge pier construction, that is pumped out to dewater the work area.

CONSIDÉRE HINGE — A construction detail used to reduce built-in bending stresses in reinforced-concrete arch ribs. The Considére Hinge, named for French engineer Armand Considére, is a temporary hinge that is reinforced and closed with a concrete pour after the dead load is applied to the arches.

CREEP — The tendency of concrete to change dimensions slightly under long-term loading.

DEAD LOAD — The self-weight of the bridge components.

DECK — The portion of the bridge structure that provides a roadway surface to carry traffic.

DECK ARCH — An arch bridge structure type with its deck supported by spandrel columns above arch ribs. *The arch is located below the road deck.*

DECK GIRDER — *A large beam, made of concrete, steel, or wood, within the road deck that spans between the structure's main supports.*

DOLPHIN — Structure independent of bridge used to protect bridge piers against errant vessels and drift.

DONKEY — A steam-powered hoisting engine, mounted on skids

〜〜〜〜

with a vertical boiler and equipped to haul in one or more wire ropes, commonly used in logging. Bridge contractors found donkeys useful when they improvised cranes, pile drivers, and other equipment.

DRAWREST — *Another name for large structures (fenders) that protect bridge piers.*

FALSEWORK — Temporary structure used to support concrete forms during construction.

FENDER — Structure to protect bridge piers against errant vessels and drift.

FREYSSINET METHOD — A method of reinforced-concrete arch construction in which a short section of the arch ribs is temporarily left open at the crown, then jacks are placed in the openings and the arch rib segments are jacked away from each other just enough to compensate for creep and shrinkage of the concrete, shortening due to dead loads, and stresses caused by temperature changes. After jacking, the reinforcement from each segment of arch rib is connected and the crown of the arch is closed with a final concrete pour.

HANGER — Structure member that transfers loads from the roadway deck to the arch rib in a tied arch type bridge.

HYDROSTATIC PRESSURE — Pressure caused by the weight of a fluid such as water above and around a submerged structure, acting in all directions and tending to collapse submerged structures.

LIVE LOAD — Weight of vehicles, persons, and cargoes carried by the bridge.

OBELISK — *A tall four-sided structure of stone or concrete, tapering to a pyramidal point (see Siuslaw River Bridge).*

OCZMA — Oregon Coastal Zone Management Association

OCHA — Oregon Coast Highway Association

ODOT — Oregon Department of Transportation

OSHC — Oregon State Highway Commission

OSHD — Oregon State Highway Department

PALLADIAN — A Renaissance architectural style originated by Andrea Palladio.

PIER — Vertical structure supporting the spans of a bridge, typically in water.

PILE/PILING — Long, slender foundation component, typically timber, driven into the soil.

PORTAL — The entryway from open roadway into an overhead bridge structure.

PRE-STRESSED CONCRETE — Concrete components strengthened by providing reinforcement that is under stress when the concrete is cast. Pre-stressing increases a component's load-carrying capacity and its durability.

PYLONS — *Tall decorative structures marking the entrance to a bridge or drive through segments of the bridge.*

REINFORCED-CONCRETE DECK GIRDER — Bridge structure type with girders and floor beams cast integrally with the roadway deck.

RIPRAP — Large rock placed around bridge piers and other underwater structures to protect them from the scouring action of rivers and tides, which tends to undermine foundations.

SEAL — First layer of concrete poured at the bottom of piers to seal water out of the cofferdam.

SHEET PILING — Wooden planks or corrugated steel driven into soil, typically used to construct cofferdams and retaining walls.

SHORING — Temporary structure provided to prevent collapse of cofferdams or excavations during construction.

SHRINKAGE — The tendency of concrete to shrink slightly as it cures and ages.

SPAN — Distance between vertical supports.

SPANDREL COLUMN — Structure member that transfers loads from the roadway deck to the arch rib in a deck arch type bridge.

STRESS — Force per unit area carried by a structural member. Bridge designers size structural members so that the stresses due to loads the bridge must resist are less than allowable stress values for the material.

SUBSTRUCTURE — The foundation and supports of a bridge that carries the weight of the superstructure to the ground.

SUPERSTRUCTURE — The horizontal part of the bridge that spans the supports and carries the traffic across. It also passes its weight and that of the traffic to the substructure.

SWING-TYPE DRAWBRIDGE — Movable bridge type, having one span that pivots around a central pier providing two navigation channels (see Umpqua River Bridge).

TEMPERATURE STRESSES — Stresses induced in a structure by temperature changes when portions of a structure are prevented from expanding or contracting freely.

TIED ARCH — An arch bridge structure type in which the deck resists the tendency of the arch ribs to push their piers apart. Hangers support the deck from the arch ribs.

TRUNNION — The balance point on which a bascule bridge pivots. On one side the road deck rises to allow passage of a tall vessel on the water below and on the other side a counterweight lowers deeper into the pier housing to counter the weight of the lifting road deck. The process is reversed to lower the road deck (see Siuslaw River Bridge).

VIADUCT — A bridge over land that usually has many short- or medium-length spans.

Bibliography

Book I

Part I

Introduction

• *Books*

BLAKELY, JOE R. *Lifting Oregon Out of the Mud.* Wallowa, Oregon: Bear Creek Press, 2006

BOTTENBERG, RAY. *Bridges of the Oregon Coast.* Arcadia Publishing, 2006

STERNBRIDGE JR., JAMES (Editor) *Pathfinder: The First Automobile Trip From Newport to Siletz Bay, July 1912.* Newport, Oregon: Lincoln County Historical Society

WYATT, STEVE. *Bayfront Book.* Newport, Oregon: Lincoln County Historical Society, 2003

• *Articles*

HADLOW, ROBERT W. "C.B. McCullough, The Engineer and Oregon's Bridge Building Boom, 1919–1936." *Pacific Northwest Quarterly* (January 1991)

HUSING, ONNO (Director OCZMA). "A History of U.S. Highway 101." *Oregon Coastal Notes,* Oregon Coastal Zone Management Association (March 2008 newsletter)

LIPIN, LAWRENCE M. "Cast Aside the Automobile Enthusiast, Class Conflict, Tax Policy, and the Preservation of Nature in Progressive Era Oregon." *Oregon Historical Quarterly* (Summer 2006/Volume 107, Number 2)

• *Online*

Oregon Blue Book (http://bluebook.state.or.us/cultural/history/history23.htm)

Chapter 1

• *Book*

PURSLEY, ED. *The Florence Book.* Florence, Oregon: Siuslaw Pioneer Museum, 2008

• *Articles*

SULLIVAN, ARTHUR D. "The Roosevelt Highway, Log of the First Automobile Trip from Astoria to Crescent City by Way of a New Road." *The Sunday Oregonian* (September 26, 1926)

SULLIVAN, ARTHUR D. "The Roosevelt Highway, The Log of the Road from Reedsport to Crescent City." *The Sunday Oregonian* (October 3, 1926)

• *Oral History*

DERRICKSON, T.M. (RICKI) (December 31, 1995)

Chapter 2

• *Articles*

BARBER, LAWRENCE. "58 Years Ago, Daring Drivers Took to Roosevelt Coast Highway." *The Sunday Oregonian* (October 25, 1987)

MILES, EDNA. "Glenada Changes." *50th Anniversary Edition 1920–*

Bibliography

1970 Siuslaw Pioneer Series, Siuslaw Pioneer Museum (1970)

NORDAHL, ANDY "I Remember When." *Siuslaw News* (February 27, 2008)

• *Research Paper*

BRALEY, CHERYL. "The Siuslaw River Bridge: A Vital Link" (July 21, 1994)

• *Oral History*

DERRICKSON, T.M. (RICKI) (December 31, 1995)

JENSEN, FRED (July 20008)

MERZ, BOB (June 16, 2006)

SAUBERT, JACK (2006)

Chapter 3

• *Book*

HADLOW, ROBERT W. *Elegant Arches, Soaring Spans*. Corvallis: Oregon State University Press, 2001

• *Articles*

"All Ferries Show Increasing Traffic." *The Siuslaw Oar* (September 20, 1935)

HADLOW, ROBERT W. "C.B. McCullough, The Engineer and Oregon's Bridge-Building Boom, 1919–1936." *Pacific Northwest Quarterly* (January 1991)

HUSING, ONNO (Director OCZMA). "A History of U.S. Highway 101." *Oregon Coastal Notes*, Oregon Coastal Zone Management Association (March 2008 newsletter)

"Nearly 1,100 Cars Cross Ferry Sunday." *The Siuslaw Oar* (September 7, 1934)

"That Bridge." *The Siuslaw Oar.* (September 1, 1933)

"Traffic Picking Up on the Coast Highway." *The Siuslaw Oar* (May 18, 1934)

• *ODOT Report*

State Highway Commission Yaquina Bay Bridge & Oregon Coast Highway Statistics (September 30, 1936)

• *Online*

questia.com. Timeline results for Oregon history, Oregon Coast Highway Association

Part II
Chapter 4

• *Books*

HADLOW, ROBERT W. *Elegant Arches, Soaring Spans*. Corvallis: Oregon State University Press, 2001

SMITH, DWIGHT A, JAMES B. NORMAN, PIETER T. DYKMAN. *Historic*

Bibliography

Highway Bridges of Oregon. Portland: Oregon Historical Society Press, 1989

• *Articles*

EDMONSTON JR., GEORGE P. "Coastal Jewels." *Oregon Stater*, OSU Alumni Association (December 1999)

HADLOW, ROBERT W. "C.B. McCullough, The Engineer and Oregon's Bridge-Building Boom, 1919–1936." *Pacific Northwest Quarterly* (January 1991)

HUSING, ONNO (Director OCZMA). "A History of U.S. Highway 101." *Oregon Coastal Notes*, Oregon Coastal Zone Management Association (March 2008 newsletter)

• *ODOT Resource*

HADLOW, ROBERT. W., Senior Historian

Chapter 5

• *Book*

HADLOW, ROBERT W. *Elegant Arches, Soaring Spans*. Corvallis: Oregon State University Press, 2001

• *Articles*

EDMONSTON JR., GEORGE P. "Coastal Jewels." *Oregon Stater*, OSU Alumni Association (December 1999)

HADLOW, ROBERT W. "C.B. McCullough, The Engineer and Oregon's Bridge-Building Boom, 1919–1936." *Pacific Northwest Quarterly* (January 1991)

HUSING, ONNO (Director OCZMA). "A History of U.S. Highway 101." *Oregon Coastal Notes*, Oregon Coastal Zone Management Association (March 2008 newsletter)

Chapter 6

• *Book*

HADLOW, ROBERT W. *Elegant Arches, Soaring Spans*. Corvallis: Oregon State University Press, 2001

• *Articles*

HADLOW, ROBERT W. "C.B. McCullough, The Engineer and Oregon's Bridge-Building Boom, 1919–1936." *Pacific Northwest Quarterly* (January 1991)

HUSING, ONNO (Director OCZMA). "A History of U.S. Highway 101." *Oregon Coastal Notes*, Oregon Coastal Zone Management Association (March 2008 newsletter)

Part III

Chapter 7

• *Book*

HADLOW, ROBERT W. *Elegant Arches, Soaring Spans*. Corvallis: Oregon State University Press, 2001

Bibliography

〜〜

• *Articles*

HADLOW, ROBERT W. "C.B. McCullough, The Engineer and Oregon's Bridge-Building Boom, 1919–1936." *Pacific Northwest Quarterly* (January 1991)

HUSING, ONNO (Director OCZMA). "A History of U.S. Highway 101." *Oregon Coastal Notes*, Oregon Coastal Zone Management Association (March 2008 newsletter)

• *Research Paper and Project*

ATLY, ELIZABETH SHELLIN. "C.B. McCullough and The Oregon Coastal Bridges Project," for Architecture 430: American Utilitarian Architecture (June 3, 1977)

LINK, GARY. "Oregon Historic Bridge Recording Project." Historic American Engineering Record (HAER–58, 1990)

• *Note*

IVAN MERCHANT quote from Hadlow book originally came from interview of LOUIS F. PIERCE with MERCHANT on June 4, 1980, transcript held by PIERCE, Junction City, Oregon

Chapter 8

• *Book*

HADLOW, ROBERT W. *Elegant Arches, Soaring Spans*. Corvallis: Oregon State University Press, 2001

• *Articles*

EDMONSTON JR., GEORGE P. "Coastal Jewels." *Oregon Stater*, OSU Alumni Association (December 1999)

HADLOW, ROBERT W. "C.B. McCullough, The Engineer and Oregon's Bridge-Building Boom, 1919–1936." *Pacific Northwest Quarterly* (January 1991)

• *Research Project*

LINK, GARY. "Oregon Historic Bridge Recording Project" Historic American Engineering Record (HAER–58, 1990)

Chapter 9

• *Book*

HADLOW, ROBERT W. *Elegant Arches, Soaring Spans*. Corvallis: Oregon State University Press, 2001

• *Articles*

FIEDLER, JOHN. "Turning 65," *Siuslaw News* (March 2001)

"Five Coast Bridges Get O.K. by P.W.A." *The Siuslaw Oar* (January 12, 1934)

HUSING, ONNO (Director OCZMA). "A History of U.S. Highway 101." *Oregon Coastal Notes*, Oregon Coastal Zone Management Association (March 2008 newsletter)

• *Online*

"Public Works Administration." *Wikipedia.org* (Primary Source *America Builds: The Record of PWA*, Public Works Administration, Division of Information)

Bibliography

Chapter 10

• *Articles*

HADLOW, ROBERT W. "C.B. McCullough, The Engineer and Oregon's Bridge-Building Boom, 1919–1936." *Pacific Northwest Quarterly* (January 1991)

"Highway Ass'n in Meet at Newport" (October 26, 1934), "Bridges on Coast to be Toll Free" (February 22, 1935), "Toll Free Bridges Finally Assured" (June 28, 1935), *The Siuslaw Oar*

• *Research Project*

LINK, GARY. "Oregon Historic Bridge Recording Project" Historic American Engineering Record (HAER–58, 1990)

Part IV
Chapter 11

• *Book*

HADLOW, ROBERT W. *Elegant Arches, Soaring Spans*. Corvallis: Oregon State University Press, 2001

• *Articles*

BALDOCK, ROBERT H. "Bridge Builders' Secrets: State highway engineer reveals construction problems faced in spanning Oregon's coast inlets." *The Oregon Motorist, Vol XVI, No 1* (May 1936)

CALDER, BILL. "Condie Balcom McCullough Oregon's Master Bridge Builder," *Oregon Coast* magazine (June/July 1986)

CHASE, ORRIN C. "Design of Coast Highway Bridges." *Civil Engineering, Vol. 6, No.10* (October 1936)

"Condic McCullough was the Man in Charge," Celebrating the 50th Anniversary of the Florence Siuslaw River Bridge. *Siuslaw News* (booklet) page 19 (May 1986)

Editorial. *Statesman*. Salem (March 31, 1936)

HADLOW, ROBERT W. "C.B. McCullough, The Engineer and Oregon's Bridge-Building Boom, 1919–1936." *Pacific Northwest Quarterly* (January 1991)

PAXSON, GLENN S. "Construction of Coast Highway Bridges." *Civil Engineering, Vol. 6, No.10* (October 1936)

Chapter 12

• *Books*

BOTTENBERG, RAY. *Bridges of the Oregon Coast*. Arcadia Publishing, 2006

CORTRIGHT, ROBERT S. *Bridging: Discovering the Beauty of Bridges*. Bridge Ink, Tigard, Oregon, 1998

WYATT, STEVE. *Bayfront Book*. Newport, Oregon: Lincoln County Historical Society, 2003

• *Articles*

BALDOCK, ROBERT H. "Bridge Builders' Secrets: State highway engineer reveals construction problems faced in spanning Oregon's

Bibliography

coast inlets." *The Oregon Motorist, Vol XVI, No 1* (May 1936)

HUSING, ONNO (Director OCZMA). "A History of U.S. Highway 101." *Oregon Coastal Notes.* Oregon Coastal Zone Management Association (March 2008 newsletter)

McCULLOUGH, C.B. (Bridge Engineer) & R.A. FURROW (Resident Engineer). "Yaquina Bay Bridge." *The Oregon Motorist, Vol XVI, No 1* (May 1936)

Two articles about dedication. *Port Umpqua Courier.* Reedsport (October 1936)

• *ODOT Reports*

Letter reporting final expenses on all bridges (February 23, 1938)

PAXSON, GLENN S. (Bridge Project Superintendent in McCullough's absence). Weekly reports (January 1936–September 1936)

State Highway Commission Yaquina Bay Bridge & Oregon Coast Highway Statistics (September 30, 1936)

Yaquina Bay Bridge statistics

• *Online*

http://generalconstructionco.com. History of General Construction Company

http://greatwesterncorp.biz. Cathodic protection work

Chapter 13

• *Books*

BLAKELY, JOE R. *Lifting Oregon Out of the Mud.* Wallowa, Oregon: Bear Creek Press, 2006

BOTTENBERG, RAY. *Bridges of the Oregon Coast.* Arcadia Publishing, 2006

CORTRIGHT, ROBERT S. *Bridging: Discovering the Beauty of Bridges.* Bridge Ink, Tigard, Oregon, 1998

SMITH, DWIGHT A, JAMES B. NORMAN, PIETER T. DYKMAN. *Historic Highway Bridges of Oregon.* Portland: Oregon Historical Society Press, 1989

• *Articles*

BALDOCK, ROBERT H. "Bridge Builders' Secrets: State highway engineer reveals construction problems faced in spanning Oregon's coast inlets." *The Oregon Motorist, Vol XVI, No 1* (May 1936)

McCULLOUGH, C.B. (Bridge Engineer) & MARSHALL DRESSER (Resident Engineer). "Alsea Bay Bridge," *The Oregon Motorist, Vol XVI, No 1* (May 1936)

OWENS, LYNNE LaREAU. "Waldport's Alsea Bay Bridge: The Second Time Around." *Oregon Coast* magazine (July/August 1991)

SCHMIDT, CURTIS M. "Bridge Dedication: 1936." *Oregon Coast* magazine (July/August 1991)

• *ODOT Reports*

Alsea Bay Bridge statistics

Bibliography

Letter reporting final expenses on all bridges (February 23, 1938)

Paxson, Glenn S. (Bridge Project Superintendent in McCullough's absence). Weekly reports (January 1936–September 1936)

• *U.S. Department of Transportation Notice*

1992 Biennial Awards Winner

• *Online*

http://Oregon.gov/ODOT New bridge information

Chapter 14

• *Books*

Bottenberg, Ray. *Bridges of the Oregon Coast.* Arcadia Publishing, 2006

Smith, Dwight A, James B. Norman, Pieter T. Dykman. *Historic Highway Bridges of Oregon.* Portland: Oregon Historical Society Press, 1989

• *Articles*

Calder, Bill. "Condie Balcom McCullough Oregon's Master Bridge Builder." *Oregon Coast* magazine (June/July 1986)

McCullough, C.B. (Bridge Engineer) & Arthur Jordan (Resident Engineer). "Siuslaw River Bridge." *The Oregon Motorist, Vol XVI, No 1* (May 1936)

"Siuslaw Bridge Opening." *Port Umpqua Courier,*" Reedsport (April 3, 1936)

Chapter 15

• *Books*

Bottenberg, Ray. *Bridges of the Oregon Coast.* Arcadia Publishing, 2006

Smith, Dwight A, James B. Norman, Pieter T. Dykman. *Historic Highway Bridges of Oregon.* Portland: Oregon Historical Society Press, 1989

• *Articles*

McCullough, C.B. (Bridge Engineer) & D.R.Smith and L.L. Jensen (Resident Engineers). "Umpqua River Bridge." *The Oregon Motorist, Vol XVI, No 1* (May 1936)

Numerous articles. *Port Umpqua Courier,* Reedsport (April 1934–September 1936)

• *ODOT Reports*

Letter reporting final expenses on all bridges (February 23, 1938)

Paxson, Glenn S. (Bridge Project Superintendent in McCullough's absence). Weekly reports (January 1936–September 1936)

Umpqua River Bridge statistics

• *Online*

http://en.wikipedia.org/wiki/List_of_bridges_on_U.S._Route_101_in_Oregon

Bibliography

Chapter 16

• *Books*

BLAKELY, JOE R. *Lifting Oregon Out of the Mud*. Bear Creek Press, Wallowa, Oregon, 2006

BOTTENBERG, RAY. *Bridges of the Oregon Coast*. Arcadia Publishing, 2006

PLOWDEN, DAVID. *Bridges: The Spans of North America*. W.W. Norton & Company (revised edition), 2001

SMITH, DWIGHT A, JAMES B. NORMAN, PIETER T. DYKMAN. *Historic Highway Bridges of Oregon*. Portland: Oregon Historical Society Press, 1989

• *Articles*

CHASE, ORRIN C. "Design of Coast Highway Bridges." *Civil Engineering, Vol. 6, No.10* (October 1936)

"History of work on local bridges." *The World* newspaper. Coos Bay (August 3, 2007)

LANDES, CHERYL. "McCullough Bridge; Engineering as Art." *Oregon Coast* magazine (July/August 1991)

McCULLOUGH, C.B. (Bridge Engineer) & RAYMOND ARCHIBALD and D.R. SMITH (Resident Engineers). "Coos Bay Bridge." *The Oregon Motorist, Vol XVI, No 1* (May 1936)

MUSICAR, JESSICA. "McCullough Bridge slated for work." *The World* newspaper. Coos Bay (February 22, 2007)

MUSICAR, JESSICA. "Bridge work moves on." *The World* newspaper. Coos Bay (February 5, 2009)

Numerous articles. *Port Umpqua Courier*. Reedsport (mid-March 1936–mid-June 1936)

• *ODOT Reports*

Coos Bay Bridge statistics

Letter reporting final expenses on all bridges, (February 23, 1938)

PAXSON, GLENN S. (Bridge Project Superintendent in McCullough's absence). Weekly reports (January 1936–September 1936)

• *Online*

http://bridgehunter.com/or/coos/mccullough

Epilogue

• *Books*

HADLOW, ROBERT W. *Elegant Arches, Soaring Spans*. Corvallis: Oregon State University Press, 2001

SMITH, DWIGHT A, JAMES B. NORMAN, PIETER T. DYKMAN. *Historic Highway Bridges of Oregon*. Portland: Oregon Historical Society Press, 1989

• *Articles*

HADLOW, ROBERT W. "C.B. McCullough, The Engineer and Oregon's Bridge-Building Boom, 1919–1936." *Pacific Northwest Quarterly*

Bibliography

〰〰〰

(January 1991)

Husing, Onno (Director OCZMA). "A History of U.S. Highway 101." *Oregon Coastal Notes*, Oregon Coastal Zone Management Association (March 2008 newsletter)

• *ODOT Resource*

Hadlow, Robert W., Senior Historian

Book II
Part I
Chapter 1

• *Book*

Traylor, Ellen. *A Bridge Back*. Port Hole Publications, 2008

• *Articles*

"Buy Dirt to Make Fill at Bridge Site" (Late spring), "Bridge Work Will Begin in Few Days" (July 13, 1934), "Moving Buildings Here is Completed" (July 27, 1934), "Bridge Equipment on Its Way Here" (August 3, 1934), "Trucks Make Time on Surfacing Job" (August 10, 1934), "First Piling Driven for Siuslaw Span" (August 10, 1934), "Machinery Arrives for Building Bridge" (August 31, 1934), "Need for More Homes" (August 31, 1934), "Building of Bridge is Well Under Way" (September 14, 1934), "Old Time Drivers Doing New Work" (November 30, 1934). *The Siuslaw Oar*

Fleagle, Judy. "Working on the Bridge." *Siuslaw News Our Town*, Part

Two (Centennial supplement, April 1993)

"Right of Way for Coast Highway in Florence Obtained," *The Register–Guard*, Eugene (November 11, 1933)

• *Oral History*

Jensen, Fred (July 2008)

Chapter 2

• *Book*

Bottenberg, Ray. *Bridges of the Oregon Coast*. Arcadia Publishing, 2006.

• *Articles*

"Building of Bridge is Well Under Way" (September 14, 1934), "Bridge Workers Make Fine Progress" (September 21, 1934), "Work on Bridge Going Ahead Fine" (September 28, 1934), "Bridge Work Up to Expectations" (October 26, 1934), "Sea Diver at Work on Bridge Piers" (November 16, 1934), "Pick and Shovel in Sinking for Piers" (November 23, 1934), "To Pour Concrete for Bridge Piers" (December 7, 1934), "Concrete Pouring Began Yesterday" (December 14, 1934), "Concrete Base for First Pier is Done" (December 21, 1934), "Big Concrete Pour to Come Up Soon" (December 28, 1934), "Bridge Work to Start Florence Side" (March 1, 1935), "Falls in Cofferdam, Shoulder Broken" (March 1, 1935), "Progress Amazing on Bridge Work" (March 22, 1935), "Pouring Concrete on Florence Side" (May 10, 1935), ""Clever Work Job on Siuslaw Bridge" (September 13, 1935).t *The Siuslaw Oar*

Bibliography

〜〜〜

Chapter 3

• *Books*

BOTTENBERG, RAY. *Bridges of the Oregon Coast.* Arcadia Publishing, 2006.

DUPRE, JUDITH. *Bridges: A History of the World's Most Famous and Important Spans.* Black Dog & Leventhal Publishers, 1997

HADLOW, ROBERT W. *Elegant Arches, Soaring Spans.* Corvallis: Oregon State University Press, 2001

• *Articles*

CALDER, BILL. "Siuslaw River Bridge Celebrates 50 Years" *Siuslaw News* (May 1986)

FIEDLER, JOHN. "Turning 65," *Siuslaw News* (March 2001)

"Progress Amazing on Bridge Work" (March 22, 1935), "Riveting Hammer at Work on Bridge" (May 31, 1935), "Bridge Work on Florence Side Now" (September 6, 1935), "Only Two More Loads Bridge Steel" (October 25, 1935), "Bridge Crew Does a Big Day's Work" (November 1, 1935), "First Crossing is Made Over River" (November 22, 1935), "Final Big Pour is on Siuslaw Bridge" (January 3, 1936), "Bridge Beacons to Aid Planes' Flights" (March 13, 1936) "Concrete Pouring on Bridge is Last" (March 6, 1936). *The Siuslaw Oar*

"Traffic Now Crossing New Coast Bridge" *Portland Journal* (April 1, 1936)

• *ODOT Reports 1936*

PAXSON, GLENN S. (Bridge Project Superintendent in McCullough's absence). Weekly reports January 1936–September 1936

Siuslaw River Bridge statistics

• *ODOT Resources*

JOHNSON, DAVID, Lead Electrical Engineer (2009)

NEAL, NATE, Inspector. Siuslaw River Bridge tour and interview (August 26, 2010)

• *Research Paper*

ATLY, ELIZABETH SHELLIN. "C.B. McCullough and The Oregon Coastal Bridges Project," for Architecture 430: American Utilitarian Architecture (June 3, 1977)

• *Oral History*

FOSSEK, WALT (February 25, 2010)

GALLO, GOODREN (March 30, 2008)

JENSEN, FRED (July 2008)

TATUM, ED (Interview with DICK SMITH, 50th anniversary celebration, 1986)

Bibliography

〰️

Chapter 4

• *Book*

Dupre, Judith. *Bridges: A History of the World's Most Famous and Important Spans.* Black Dog & Leventhal Publishers, 1997

• *Articles*

"Bridge Dedication" (January 17, 1936), "Executive Committee Chosen for Bridge Dedication Fete" (March 13, 1936), "Approaches for Fill Local Job" (March 20, 1936), "Bridge Opened Tuesday Noon" (April 3, 1936), "Dedication Plans Receive Impetus" (April 3, 1936), "Ex-Governor Will Be Invited to Speak; Queen Contest is Opened" (April 17, 1936), "The Bridge" a poem (April 17, 1936), "Bridge Fete Crowd is at Eugene Today" (April 24, 1936), "Why Hurry — It is a Bridge" (May 1, 1936), "Celebration Only Two Weeks Away" (May 8, 1936), "Finest Coast Span Dedication May 24" (May 15, 1936), "Dedication Program" (May 22, 1936), "Florence is Host This Weekend at Big Double Event" (May 22, 1936), "Finest Bridge on Coast Auspiciously Dedicated" (May 29, 1936), "The Men Behind the Scene" (May 29, 1936). *The Siuslaw Oar*

"Dedication of $500,000 Siuslaw Bridge" (May 17, 1936) *The Register–Guard*

"Ferry Toots Swan Song: Bridge Open" (March 31, 1936), "Traffic Now Crossing New Coast Bridge" (April 1, 1936), "Great Throng Views Bridge Dedication" (May 25, 1936). *Portland Journal*

Fetters, Eric. "Siuslaw River Bridge Spans 60 Years" (April 3, 1996), Nordahl, Andy. "I Remember When" (February 27, 2008).

Siuslaw News

"Florence Plans Bridge Jubilee" (April 4, 1936) *Corvallis Gazette-Times*

McCullough, C.B. (Bridge Engineer) & Arthur Jordan (Resident Engineer). "Siuslaw River Bridge." *The Oregon Motorist, Vol XVI, No 1* (May 1936)

• *ODOT Resources*

Johnson, David, Lead Electrical Engineer

• *Oral History*

Gallo, Goodren (March 30, 2008)

Part II
Chapter 5

• *Articles*

Calder, Bill. "Siuslaw River Bridge Celebrates 50 Years." *Siuslaw News* (May 1986)

"Grading of North Approach is Done." *The Siuslaw Oar* (July 27, 1934)

Miles, Edna. "Glenada Changes." *Siuslaw Pioneer Series: 50th Anniversary Edition 1920–1970*, Siuslaw Pioneer Museum

Say, Harold B. "Progress Takes Its Toll." *The Oregon Motorist, Vol XVI, No 1* (May 1936)

Bibliography

〜〜〜

• *Research Paper*

BRALEY, CHERYL. "The Siuslaw River Bridge: A Vital Link" (July 21, 1994)

• *Oral History*

BARRETT, FRANK (February 18, 2010)

GALLO, GOODREN (March 30, 2008)

JENSEN, FRED (July 20008)

ZIEMER, ZANE (2008)

Chapter 6

• *ODOT Resources*

BELL, CHRISTOPHER, Historian

HADLOW, ROBERT W., Senior Historian

• *Oral History*

BARRETT, FRANK (February 18, 2010)

FOSSEK, WALT (February 25, 2010)

Chapter 7

• *Articles*

DIAMOND, ELLIOT. "Bridges 101: Southern Oregon Coast." *The Sunday Oregonian* (December 18, 1994)

MARTIN, KARROL. "On Your Mark: First over the bridge." *Siuslaw News Our Town, Part One* (Centennial supplement April 14, 1993)

"Siuslaw Bridge gains historic register status." *Siuslaw News* (November 19, 2005)

SLOAN, GENE. "10 Great Places to cross the water." *USA Today* (October 15, 1999)

• *Oral History*

BARRETT, FRANK (February 18, 2010)

FOSSEK, WALT (February 25, 2010)

HAMMON, CHIC (January 16, 2011)

JENSEN, FRED (July 2008)

UNSER, LYNN (June 26, 2010)

WELLS, DUKE (January 19, 2011)

Part III

Chapter 8

• *Articles*

FIEDLER, JOHN. "Turning 65." *Siuslaw News* (March 2001)

"Piling Replaced." *Siuslaw News* (February 27, 1969)

RUSSELL, MICHAEL. "ODOT; Siuslaw River Bridge malfunction causes massive delays on U.S. 101." *The Oregonian* (February 27, 2009)

Bibliography

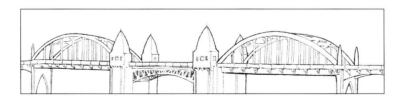

"Work begins to modernize Siuslaw River Bridge." ODOT press release (May 28, 2009)

• *Interviews*

BRUBAKER, PHIL, Mayor of Florence (August 2010)

HOAGLAND, LORETTA (February 2010)

• *ODOT Resources*

BEATTY, RON, Ona Beach bridge crew coordinator. Interview (September 22, 2010)

NEAL, NATE, inspector. Siuslaw River Bridge tour and interview (August 26, 2010)

Chapter 9

• *Articles*

BACON, LARRY. "Cape Creek Bridge becomes electrified." *The Register–Guard* (January 23, 1992)

"Oregon Bridges to Get High Tech Treatment." *Transporter*, News Room USDOT News (2004)

• *Online*

http://greatwesterncorp.biz. "Cathodic Protection: The Basics & The Tasks," Great Western Corporation

• *Interviews*

BETZ, JACQUE, Assistant City Manager of Florence (August 2010)

BRUBAKER, PHIL, Mayor of Florence (August 2010)

NELSON, FRANK, former ODOT engineer and then senior supervising engineer with Parsons Brinckerhoff in Seattle (May 2008)

• *Florence Resource*

The Central Oregon Coast Telephone Book

• *ODOT Resources*

BENNISON, TED, inspector, and ROBERT MCGILL, job foreman with contractor Great Western Corporation. McCullough Bridge tour and interview (August 30, 2010)

Index

~~~

Index

Index

~~~~~

Index

Index

Index

Index

~~~

Index

Crossing Over

A loaded log truck rumbles across the Siuslaw River Bridge toward Florence. In the days before the coastal bridges, logs were skidded with horses down to the river, linked together to form rafts, and floated on the river to numerous mills up and down stream from the logging sites.

Acknowledgments

〜〜〜

I WISH TO THANK the following people who helped immeasurably in my research:

• PEARL and LOUIS CAMPBELL — Siuslaw Pioneer Museum

• ROBERT HADLOW, PAT SOLOMON, CHRIS LEEDHAM, and CANDACE STITCH — Oregon Department of Transportation

• JODI WEEBER — Oregon Coast History Center

• CHERYL ROFFE — Lane County Historical Society

• MIKKI TINT — Oregon Historical Society

• MIKE RIVERS — Oregon Parks & Recreation Department

• HARRIET SMITH and HAROLD G. VANRIPER

— Dick Smith —

I WISH TO THANK the following:

• ROBERT W. HADLOW, Senior Historian with ODOT, for looking over the manuscript and offering valuable suggestions and additional material — author *Elegant Arches, Soaring Spans: C.B. McCullough, Oregon's Master Bridge Builder*

• RAY BOTTENBERG who fact-checked certain chapters and granted permission to quote from his book and to use his Glossary in its entirety — author *Bridges of the Oregon Coast*

• CANDICE STICH, DAVID JOHNSON, BENJAMIN TANG, and CHRIS BELL for responding to endless questions and fact-checking — Oregon Department of Transportation (ODOT)

• NATE NEAL and TED BENNISON for taking me on tours of Siuslaw River and McCullough bridges respectively and for fact-checking — ODOT

• TOM OHREN for providing historic photos — ODOT

• FRANK NELSON for explaining cathodic protection and its history — former ODOT Bridge Preservation Engineering Manager

• ROBERT MAGILL who accompanied me on tour of McCullough Bridge — Great Western Corporation, North Bend

• FRED JENSEN, FRANK BARRETT, WALT FOSSEK, GOODREN GALLO, CARL KNOWLES, ZANE ZIEMER, DON BOWMAN who spent hours recounting the past — Florence area old-timers

• TAMARA VIDOS, Microforms Coordinator, for her help at the library and for locating and sending to Siuslaw Public Library microfilm of Reedsport's *Port Umpqua Courier* — Document Center, Knight Library, University of Oregon

• JODI WEEBER, Archivist, for helping me select photos and putting them on disk — Oregon Coast History Center, Newport

• FRED JENSEN, Curator, for helping me select photos and putting them on disk — Siuslaw Pioneer Museum, Florence

• SHARON WAITE and ADELE O'BOYLE for providing files for research — Siuslaw Pioneer Museum, Florence

• Editor THERESA BAER for providing files for research and photos — *Siuslaw News*, Florence

• Mayor PHIL BRUBAKER and Assistant City Manager JACQUE BETZ took time out of busy schedules for interviews — City of Florence

• ROBERT CORTRIGHT for permission to use his quote in front pages — author *Bridging: Discovering the Beauty of Bridges*

— Judy Fleagle —

Credits

ARCHITECTURAL DRAWINGS
Oregon Department of Transportation — 118, 120, 121, 187–193

COVER PHOTOGRAPHS
Front & Back Photos — Robert Serra

DEDICATION PROGRAM REPRINT
John Bartlett — 150–151

ILLUSTRATIONS
City of Florence — 183, 184
Henderson, Stu — iii, v, 210, 223
Oregon Coast magazines — i

NEWSPAPER REPRINTS
The Oregonian — 147
Portland Journal — 43

PHOTOGRAPHS
Baer, Theresa — 224
Barrett, Frank — 142, 161
Barrett, Frank (Courtesy Mary Johnston) — 112
Fleagle, Judy — 106, 139, 163, 175–178, 180–182
Hall, Marion — 185
Lincoln County Historical Society — 2, 3, 4, 5, 8, 10, 16 (Roger A. Hart), 18, 77, 79
Mihulka, Chris *(TheShutterMaster.com)* — 224
Oregon Department of Transportation — i, 1, 22, 25, 30, 36, 38–39, 57–58, 60, 62, 64, 66–67, 69–72, 74, 76, 80, 82, 86, 88, 90, 92, 94, 96, 98, 100–101, 103–105, 107, 114, 116, 123–124, 126–127, 130, 132–133, 135–136 138, 146
Oregon Department of Transportation (Courtesy *Siuslaw News*) — 20, 23, 32, 34, 128, 130, 160
Serra, Robert — ii, vii, 28, 40, 45, 48, 50–52, 54, 61, 81, 83, 109, 152, 158, 162, 164, 171, 186, 192–194, 221
Siuslaw News — 166, 169
Smith, Richard Knox, Collection — 110, 140
Siuslaw Pioneer Museum — 6, 12, 14, 46, 84, 144, 154, 157

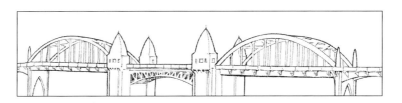

About the Author & Researcher

JUDY FLEAGLE graduated with a major in Elementary Education and a minor in English. She made good use of them by spending 22 years teaching 1st and 2nd grades in Los Gatos, California, and, after moving to Florence on the Oregon coast, spending 21 years as an editor and staff writer for *Oregon Coast* and *Northwest Travel* magazines.

Fleagle often wrote about McCullough bridges in *Oregon Coast* and during the 2005 update of the magazine's annual *Mile by Mile Guide*, she inserted information about each of McCullough's coastal bridges after they were listed on the National Register of Historic Places. She has an abiding love for these bridges and a huge respect for McCullough. Since retiring as an editor at the

Judy Fleagle

magazines, she continues as a freelance writer. Her other book, *Chuck and Jean: the Interesting Years*, was published in 1992 and dealt with her parents' remembrances.

RICHARD KNOX "DICK" SMITH graduated from Oregon State University and Yale University and has been an ordained Presbyterian Minister for the past 60 years. He has also authored *49 and Holding* and numerous articles in religious and other publications, such as *Arizona Highways* and *Oregon Coast*.

He spent an entire year researching the Siuslaw River Bridge in preparation for a Power-Point presentation to a discussion group. His research took him to Salem, Corvallis, Eugene, Eureka, California, and up and down the coast to all 12 McCullough

Dick Smith

bridges plus visits to numerous old-timers. Before he finished, his research included the back story of the highway construction, of Conde B. McCullough, and of the building of all five bridges. More than a dozen audiences saw his PowerPoint presentation, before he asked Judy Fleagle to put it into book form.

Smith's research and Fleagle's writing make the perfect team for *Crossings*. And since they each live in the Florence area, the Siuslaw River Bridge has special meaning for both of them.